Mary Morgan

Poems and Translations

Mary Morgan

Poems and Translations

ISBN/EAN: 9783744712934

Printed in Europe, USA, Canada, Australia, Japan

Cover: Foto ©Thomas Meinert / pixelio.de

More available books at **www.hansebooks.com**

Mary Morgan

Poems and Translations

ISBN/EAN: 9783744712934

Printed in Europe, USA, Canada, Australia, Japan

Cover: Foto ©Thomas Meinert / pixelio.de

More available books at **www.hansebooks.com**

POEMS

—AND—

TRANSLATIONS

—BY—

MARY MORGAN,

(GOWAN LEA.)

>   —" Das ewig Eine
> Lebt mir in Leben, sieht in meinem Sehen.
> Nichts ist denn Gott; und Gott ist nichts denn Leben.
> Gar Klar die Hülle sich vor dir erhebet.
> Dein Ich ist sie; es sterbe, was vernitchtbar;
> Und fortan lebt nur Gott in deinem Streben.
> Durchschaue, was diess Streben überlebet:
> Da wird die Hülle dir als Hülle sitchbar,
> Und unverschleirt siehst du göttlich Leben."—*Fichte*

Montreal
J. THEO. ROBINSON,
PUBLISHER.

1887

L'Envoi.

"Go, little booke, God send thee good
    passage,
And, specially, let this be thy
    prayere,
Unto them all that thee will read
    or hear:—
Where thou art wrong, after their
    help to call,
Thee to correct in any part or
    all."

OLD·POEME.

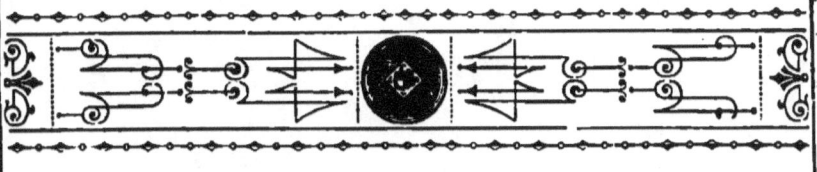

TABLE OF CONTENTS.

PART THE FIRST.

MISCELLANEOUS POEMS.   Page

To the New Year	1
Evening Hymn	2
On seeing a Procession of Nuns	3
To Nature	4
Friendship	4
The Poet's Hour	5
With a Bunch of Wild Roses	6
On the Beach	7
Tears	7
Sing on, Sweet Bird	8
One Seeing One Asleep	9
Reflections	10
In Apprehension, so like a God!	11
An Autumn Song	12
The Afterglow	13
To Mother Nature	14
The World's Teachers	15
Dreams	16
The Message	17
The New Year	18
I had a Little Flower	19
Summum Bonum	20
Charity	20
On Seeing a Child fall Asleep	21
The Present and the Future	22
Spring Song	23

	Page
To the Gowan	24
Lines addressed to ——	25
The Gardener's Soliloquy	26
A Dream of Childhood	27
At Even-tide	28
Hymn	29
In Memoriam	30
Happy, Happy Flowers	31
Summer, Winter, Spring	32
Night	33
Doubt Not	34
Sea Weeds	36
Questionings	38
Wee Willie	42
Hymn. (By my Father)	48

PART THE SECOND.

SONNETS.

	Page
To the New Year	51
Ah, Rose so Sweet	52
Morning	53
The Poet	54
Friendship	55
George Eliot	56
To the Arts	57
Time	58
Ideals	59
Friendship	60
Thought	61
Read at the Golden Wedding of E. N.	62
Silence	63
Hope	64
Destiny	65

	Page
On the Death of Carlyle	66
Written whilst studying Spinoza's " Ethics "	67
Founded on a Persian Legend	68
Life's Purpose	69
O Music!	70
The Poet's Dream	71
The Ideal	72
Oblivion	73
To " Our Club "	74
The Wanderer's Dream	75
The First Snow	76
Our Guiding Star	77
So Sad, So Strange	78

PART THE THIRD.

Meditations from " Dream-Grotto "	81

PART THE FOURTH.

TRANSLATIONS.

Poet and Reader	95
Barcarolle	96
The Letter	98
The Serenade	98
Could I but go	99
My Picture This	101
Thamire to the Roses	101
Poetry	102
On the Death of a Child	102
O Say, Sweet Little Bird	103
Thou and I	104
Heart of Mine	105
Ideals	106
By the Shore	106

To the Wind	107
Resignation	108
The Wakened Rose	109
April	110
Good-night	111
Thou Everywhere	112
Spring Song	114
The Cot	114
A Poem, Thou	115
The Castle by the Sea	116
Prière	118
My Heart, I wish to ask Thee	119
Chains	120
To-morrow	121
Sonnet by Michael Angelo	122

PART THE FIFTH.

TRANSLATIONS.

German Love	127
Without a Mother	168
The Death of Raphael	172

ADDITIONAL POEMS.

Song: Tender little Rose-bud!	179
Hymn! O Reason, Wonder, Doubt!	180
Song: Forget-me-not and Clover	181
The Comrades	182
Star to Star, &c.	184

SONNETS.

Mysterious Life!	186
Still, still thy Waters now	187
Poor, little Bird	188
Swift Roll the Waters	189
Wait, trusting Heart!	190

Page

Those poor, dumb brutes 191
With Hopefulness Man tills 192
The Young Moon rises 193
Prize Thou the Kingdom 194
Good-Night! , ... 195

TO THE NEW YEAR.

Hark! is't thy step, New Year?
With sure but stealthy pace thou aye dost come;
And in thy train are gladdening gifts for some;
    O haste thee, glad New Year!

Too swift thy step, New Year!
The past had gathered friends from many lands,
And thou dost come to part their claspèd hands:
    Alas, so soon, New Year!

'O haste!' 'Delay!' New Year;—
Two prayers together rising up to Heaven:
The answer trust; for is it not God-given?
    Meet bravely the New Year!

Bid welcome the New Year!
O clear-voiced Truth, lead in the coming morn;
And gentle Charity, our lives adorn:
    Hope lives in the New Year!

EVENING HYMN.

(For Music.)

I bow my weary head,
    And fold my hands in prayer,
And trust the God of all,
    Whose love is everywhere.

This day with all its pain,
    I lay down at His feet;
To-morrow strength will come,
    To-morrow's care to meet.

Adieu ye vain regrets!
    And dark despair, adieu!
Howe'er I may have erred,
    I did the best I knew.

My heart is full of hope,
    And fearless is it, too;
Not calmer is yon star
    That shines in heaven's blue.

He gave to me my soul,
   And knows it's inmost need ;
I cannot grasp His plan ;
   To trust Him is my creed.

I bow my weary head,
   And fold my hands in prayer,
And trust the God of all,
   Whose love is everywhere.

(On seeing a procession of Nuns going into the Chapel.)

The shades of night were falling round,
   A holy silence filled the air,
The convent bell had ceased to sound,
   It was the hour of prayer.
The Sisters to the Chapel went,
   And knelt upon the altar stair
With faces bowed and penitent ;
   Laid they life's burden there ?

To pray !—Their's seemed an easy task !
   O Thou ! Thy child forgive :
Alas, *I* know not what to ask,
   Thou knowest what to give !

TO NATURE.

Nature, I would be thy child,
    Sit and worship at thy feet;
Read the truth upon thy face,
    Wait upon thine accent sweet:
I would put my hand in thine,
    Bow my head upon thy knee,
Live upon thy love alone,
    Fearless, trusting all to thee.

FRIENDSHIP.

When friend to friend hath spoken the farewell,
    And trembled at the thought that ne'er again
Perchance they two shall meet,—the magic spell
    Of sacred friendship, is it rent in twain?

From shore to shore the waves of ocean roll,
    From East to West the lonely breezes blow,
And shall not soul commune with kindred soul
    In mutual sympathetic ebb and flow?

THE POETS' HOUR.

See where the twilight draweth nigh,
    Enswathing in the fold
Of her capacious mantle grey,
    The woodland, stream, and wold !

Still deeper grows the silence, while,
    In tenderest embrace,
She clasps the Bluebell, and enveils
    The Daisy's modest face.

With mystic rite of unseen hands
    She weaves her secret spell;
Dull earth obscured, alone awhile
    With Fancy now we dwell,

And tread her airy halls of light,
    Taste her ideal bliss ;
Behold on high a cloudless sky—
    The Poet's hour is this !

WITH A BUNCH OF WILD ROSES.

Ah, deem not that this simple little flower
   Unfolded all its tender bloom in vain;
Did it not glorify a summer hour,
   And leave a sweetness in the summer rain?

Then sigh not for its transitoriness,
   Or let this thought be joined to every sigh,
That a frail blossom's passing loveliness
   Is lovelier for the thought that it **must die!**

A human life is like a precious flower.
   One cannot truly live and be in vain:
A soul of beauty—nature's grandest dower—
   Must leave a glory on the world's wide plain.

And e'en as zephyrs waft from shore to shore
   The fragrant essence of the flowery lea;
So heaven-born Truth is floating evermore,
   From age to age of our humanity,

ON THE BEACH.

So thick the mist is hanging round,
    Vast ocean is not seen;
But we may hear his rolling wave,
    And mark where he hath been.

The veil is rent! a gleam of light!
    The forest lands appear!
Again the brooding vapors dip;
    Earth looks more hopeless, drear.

As mist upon the mountain side,
    Or as the tidal flow;
So Doubt within the human breast
    Riseth and falleth low.

TEARS.

Back, back persisting tears! Why will ye flow?
Back to the founts where ye have lain so long!
I will not have ye cloud this summer hour,
I will not have ye tremble through my song.

The tears made answer dropping slowly down:—
"Think not that we are born of grief alone:
The joy of nature moves us as its woe;
'Tis joy to-day that trembles in thy tone."

SING ON, SWEET BIRD.

(For Music.)

Sing on, sweet bird, I prythee sing;
    It joys my heart to hear;
Art thou so gladsome every day—
    No clouds in all thy year?
Oft as I watch thee fly aloft
    As seeking heaven's high dome,
I envy thee thy upward flight,
    From this my earth-bound home.

Hast thou no fear? Hast thou no care?
    O teach me all thy art,
To live and sing, and, singing, soar,
    Heavenward with lightsome heart.
What though the skies be dark betimes,
    The sun must shine again;
O might I tune my notes from thine
    As if they knew no pain!

But yet if sorrow will have voice,
    Will follow my refrain,
Know, 'tis that Nature leaves no choice,
    Sad memory leads the strain.

ON SEEING ONE ASLEEP.

Sleep on! thy busy brain may rest awhile.
Far-reaching mind, unconscious of thyself—
Thy subtle genius—soundly dost thou sleep
Nor knowest aught of any presence near!
Yet is there one to guard thee tenderly,
And lay a placid hand upon thy brow,
Repelling all intrusion with a glance
And up-raised finger, as to say, "He sleeps!"

Ah! in our waking moments do we think
How much of latent power exists in us—
How many faculties are yet asleep,
Unconscious of themselves, or of the past,
Or future, or the Spirit of the worlds—
The Being that can still the noisy day,
And beckon silently unto the night
To come and give earth's weary children sleep.

REFLECTIONS.

A placid water 'tween the willow trees
Has made a mirror wherein we behold
A perfect image of the beauteous earth,
Now flushing 'neath the sunset's parting glow.
There are the water-lilies yellow, white;
The fleecy clouds which move in silence by;
The long lithe grasses sleeping on the wave,
Or lisping a low greeting to the wind;
While solitary, and with kingly grace,
An aged elm o'erlooks the quiet scene.

There is a mirror clearer than the stream;
A light conpared to which yon orb is pale;
A beauty fairer than the lily's bloom.
Awaking it to seek the life divine,
A spiritual ray illumes the soul,
Whose image is upon the ages cast,
And brightens with the steady flow of years.
O Time! stupendous mirror of the race!
Revealer of the beautiful and true!
In thee how clear th' eternal glory shines!

"In apprehension, so like a God!"—*Hamlet*,

Take the mouldering dust,
Wake it into life,—
Matter is but servant of the mind.

Touch the silent keys:
Genius can evoke
Music wherein gods commune with men.

Read the soul of man,
And the farthest star:
Truth is one, and is forever true.

Think the wildest thought,
Hope the utmost hope,—
Time shall be when all shall be fulfilled.

Wonder not at deed,
Wonder more at thought,
Wonder at the hope that feeds itself.

Genius is divine,
Genius is the true:
Man becomes that which he worships,—God!

AN AUTUMN SONG.

Cold blows the Autumn wind and drear,
   From out the lowering west;
Low wail the crimson leaves and sere
   As if they longed for rest.

Upon my heart they seem to fall,
   And stay its joyful tone,
Awaking there a plaintive call—
   The echo of their own.

O forest leaves, from yonder trees
   Borne upon languid wing,
You hear not in the wandering breeze
   The whisper of the Spring.

While far beyond the sky's dark cloud,
   I know the stars shine clear,
And that beneath the Autumn shroud
   Awaits the future year.

THE AFTERGLOW.

It is the afterglow. The dying sun
Went down behind yon distant purple hill
Where sleep the quiet dead, while breezes still
A solemn requiem chant ere day be done.
Full o'er the city yet, in beauty rare,
Shine rosy beams that touch the countless spires,
And play upon the rushing river there,
Illume the leaden sky with crimson fires]
More splendid far than when at noontide hour
The sun was in the zenith of his power.

O dead and gone—is this the afterglow!
From hidden moss-grown graves behind yon hill
A soft effulgence seemeth yet to flow—
A subtle tie that binds us closer still,
And kindles in our spirits' clouded skies
A fire of hope that never, never dies:
Bright picture unto which souls trouble-tossed
Have turned, in holy contemplation lost,
Forgetting earth's wild turmoil, hate, and strife,
To dream a dream of love's unending life.

TO MOTHER NATURE.

"Oh, pray to Him!" they say to me:
"Prayer is for all that live!"
Alas! I know not what to ask:
Thou knowest what to give.

The leaves bestrew my lonely path,
    I know not where I go;
But in yon dimly twinkling stars,
    And in this drifting snow,

Is somewhat yet that speaks to me;
    And Mother Nature's call
Is aye the voice I love to hear,
    For She is all in all.

THE WORLD'S TEACHERS.

AN IMPROMPTU.

In the dimly-lighted chamber
   Hung with crimson and with gold,
See the radiant maidens sitting,
   Dreaming of the days of old.

' Yonder,' says one, glancing upward
   To the portraits on the wall,
' Yonder are the grand old masters
   Looking down upon us all :

' Michael Angelo and Turner,
   Raphael and Socrates,
Mozart, Byron,—all the poets,—
   O that ours were days like these !

' Might we but commune in spirit
   With the great heroic band !
Might their lofty genius lift us
   Into their ideal land !

' Ah ! the tapers flicker dimly,
   Light and life burn to decay,
But the world of Art and Beauty
   Opens to an endless day.'

DREAMS.

Fairy, flowery, fleeting dreams,
Strange as moonlight's fitful gleams,
   Flitting over sorrow's night,
   Flooding it with sudden light ;
Flowers of fancy ! could ye rest
Constant in the human breast !

Wondrous, eery, wavering dreams,
Weird as hazy moonlight streams,
   Hailing from—we know not where,
   Falling softly into air,
Wandering far through worlds above,
Lost in clouds of light and love !

Weary, woful, wasting dreams,
Pensive as pale moonlight beams,
   Anxious, through some bitter loss,
   Seeking shadows of the cross,
Searching haunts of memory,
Pondering life's mystery !

*   *   *   *   *

Calm and cold—too chill for dreams;
Death o'er Life—the end—it seems;
   Cheerless sky and rayless mind—
   This, the *all* for human kind?
Moons shall rise and moons shall set,
Worlds revolving, *we* shall yet
   Dream again, and, dreaming, soar,
   Wondering, dreaming, more and more!

THE MESSAGE.
(For Music.)

Go little bird and tell my love from me,
   That I am lone without her and do mourn;
Fly pretty bird across the summer sea,
And whisper to her all I tell to thee.

Nay, tell her not! I would not that she grieve;
   I know she will not linger long away;
Our troth is plighted; she could not deceive;
So deep I love, I must in her believe.

And love like ours is to my soul so dear,
   I fain would keep it there unshaped in words;
Within my inmost heart, until she hear
The burden from my lips, when she appear!

THE NEW YEAR.

"Rejoice! it is the glad New Year, rejoice!"
This was the greeting from a cheerful voice.
The earth seemed newly decked in glistening white,
And on my window-pane the morning light
Shone through quaint landscapes; for the frost and snow
Had traced with artist hand o'er all below
(And while the human world in slumber lay)
The fairest scenes,—a wonderful array.
My fancy, too, not idle, spread its wings,
And, joyful as the lark that heavenward sings,
Upon the canvas of the untold year
Portrayed its every joy and hope and fear.

That New Year's day, with all its hope sublime,
Is garnered now into the lap of time;
The pictures on my window-pane are lost;
Ideals, too, have vanished like the frost.
How shall I now rejoice in the New Year?
Responsive in my soul, a voice spake clear:
" Rejoice, rejoice, with every birth of morn!
For with each dawn a new new-year is born;
Though airy castles fall, yet build again:
Far nobler flights the soul shall yet attain;
No losses can its majesty appall,
For time shall be till it surmount them all!"

I HAD A LITTLE FLOWER.

(TO MRS. R———, IN MEMORY OF FLORA.)

I had a little flower—fair, so fair—
    And every day it grew more purely white;
I loved my flower, and tended it with care,
    And kept it from the chilling frost of night;

And said within my heart: "Ah, tender flower,
    How shalt thou bear the stormy winter blast,
For thou wast formed to grace the summer bower,
    And ah! the summer is so nearly past!"

When autumn came, an angel stood beside
    My little flower, and marked it for his own;
I trembled for my darling and my pride,
    As sighed the desolating winter's moan.

At last, one night when earth was cold and drear,
    The loving angel took my flower away,
And placed it where no chilling wind nor sere,
    Could touch its tender blossom with decay.

The summer bowers have grown less fair for me,
    But there's a deeper radiance in the skies;
My little flower now blooms eternally;
    The angel guards it still in Paradise.

SUMMUM BONUM.

Inscribed to Felix Adler.

To live in every thought
    A life so true and pure;
To do in every deed
    The noblest, and endure;
To hate with direst hate
    The wrong and sin we see;
The sinner to restore
    With gentlest charity;—
This is the heavenly mind,
    Wherever it be found;
A soul at one with good,
    Knows only hallowed ground.

CHARITY.

Thou askest not to know the creed,
The rank, or name is naught to thee,
Where'er the human heart cries 'help!"
Thy kingdom is, O Charity!

ON SEEING A CHILD FALL ASLEEP.

The heavy eyelids slowly droop,
    The eyes grow less and less,
The last of languid glances flown,
    Has left but peacefulness.
'Twas like the twilight's mellow shades,
    That, quivering o'er the snow,
Seemed lingering glimpses from the sun,
    And almost loathe to go.

Ere long shalt thou refreshed awake,
    Nor ever know surprise,
That weariness from thee took flight,
    In such a strange, sweet guise.
As suddenly the Spring anew,
    Starts from beneath the ground,
Once more with fresh life to pursue,
    Its never-ending round.

THE PRESENT AND THE FUTURE.

Question :

    What shall the next step be?
    Know'st thou, Futurity?
    Bring answer swift to me;
    Show me my destiny.

Answer :

    What dost thou ask of me?
    Show thee thy destiny?
    No life, alas, can be
    Apart from mystery.

    I cannot reach to thee;
    My power thou may'st defy;
    Thou bringest unto me
    That which in me doth lie!

SPRING SONG.

I wandered in the well-known path,
  The sky was bright and blue,
The trees were clad in freshest green,
  The sunlight streaming through.

The nightingales were singing loud
  Their love-songs from the vale,
The purling brooklet, as it flowed
  Seemed chanting a sweet tale.

O whence this gladness in the air?
  And wherefore do ye sing?
The little birds were answering me :—
  "Rejoice, for it is spring!"

Rejoice, for it is spring! I cried;
  Rejoice for all the year!
For winter too—there is no death
  In Nature—have no fear!

And joying thus for all the year,
  More joyful could I sing
Than bird, or brooklet flowing by:
  "Rejoice, for it is spring!"

TO THE GOWAN.

[The English wild daisy is known in Scotland as the " Gowan."]

Little Gowan, Scotia's flower !
Whence hast thou that dreamful eye
Looking up into the sky,
Where the homeless clouds go by?
Little Gowan, modest, shy.

Little Gowan, poet's flower !
Once I took thee far away,
Planted thee where flowers gay
Smiled upon me all the day.
Yet I chose thee from the rest
(For old Scotland's sake the best),
In my book thy blossom pressed.

Little Gowan, poet's flower !
Couldst not thou thy hills resign?
Every day I saw thee pine
For thy country—thine and mine.
Wintry wind came driving past
Gusts of snow, and in the blast
Thou wert buried, rudely, fast.

Little Gowan, Scotia's flower !
April sun has brought to light
Crocuses and snowdrops white ;
Where thy smiling face to-night ?
Winds are wailing, sobbing low :—
"Out of reach of frost and snow
Went the Gowan long ago !"

LINES ADDRESSED TO ——,

All silently the tear drops flow,
    And tremble on thy cheek ;
As silent as the moonlight's fall
    Upon the quivering deep.

On thy young life hath sorrow left
    Already her deep stain ?
Above thee doth her spirit brood,
    Or flit to come again ?

THE GARDENER'S SOLILOQUY.

The last rays of the setting sun,
    Had fallen athwart the wold;
The last leaves of the shivering trees,
    Fell crimson now and gold.

The last wild flower had passed away,
    And left a cheerless vale;
While weirdly through the gloaming went
    The autumn wind's low wail.

By came the gardener, old and gray,
    And looked with solemn eye;
Then spake in accents trembling, low:
    "There's little left to die!"

"When youth is gone, and eye is dim,
    And memory fled for aye,
The leaves of our humanity
    Thus flutter to decay."

The old man paused, and gazed awhile
    Upon the sunset sky;
Then spake again his doleful strain:
    "There's little left to die!"

A DREAM OF CHILDHOOD.

Little star so brightly shining
    Through my window-pane to-night,
Bringing down to earth a message,
    From that distant world of light.

Would that I might read the record
    Which within thy beams doth lie,
Learn the story of the dwellers
    In that distant azure sky.

Sun and moon and stars are yonder,
    Death and life—a dual play;
This, perchance, thy ghost that wanders
    Over space to earth to-day.

Or doth further glory wait thee?
    Shalt thou distant æons see,
Be the queen of night and beauty,
    When our earth no more shall be?

Grow until thou reach a splendour,
    Which the earth hath never seen?
Be the dwelling of a nobler,
    Higher race than yet hath been?

Little star! thy brightness dazzles
    Me with many a subtle ray;
Charms my willing fancy, leads it
    O'er thy airy path away.

AT EVENTIDE.—(Song).

O hush! I hear the singing
    Of one to me so dear;
Soon as the twilight falleth,
    Her voice I seem to hear.

She comes and sits beside me,
    And soothes me with her song;
O twilight shadows, linger!
    I would the lay prolong.

But ah! the day is closing,
    The melody doth cease,
And clouded is my spirit,
    Departed is my peace.

I tarry for the morrow,
    To charm away my pain;
She cometh with the twilight,
    And I shall dream again.

HYMN.

(For Music.)

Be strong, O soul! The morning breaketh fair;
All blue the sky—no cloudlet anywhere;
Yet think,—thy path is infinite and there
    Thou walkest all alone : O soul, be strong!

Be strong, O soul! It is the full noon-day;
But thorns and briars have sprung up on thy way;
Take heed unto thy steps, that so thou may
    Not faint nor fall : do thou beware, O soul!

Be strong, O soul! The night comes on apace,
The crescent moon hath hid her pensive face,
Nor canst thou on the darkening heavens trace
    One lonely star : now, now be strong, O soul!

Be calm, O soul! Dream not the night can last :
If memory hath linked thee to the past,
So, to the future, Hope hath bound thee fast :
    Be thou as calm as strong, O anxious soul!

IN MEMORIAM.

(To Mrs. E. M. T.)

Mother :
  Take up thy harp, my child, and play to me
  Once more the old familiar melody,
  For as I hear the strain I feel that thou
  Art mine indeed, and read upon thy brow
  The sweet communion of our inmost thought.
  With thee alway beside me there is naught
  I cannot bear—the envy or the blame
  Of multitudes, for thou art still the same,
  Through woe or weal. My daughter, can it be
  That thou dost feel all that I feel for thee?

Daughter :
  O mother, hearken while I touch the keys,
  And wake the gentle tones I know will please
  Thy tender heart ; and if a time shall come,
  When these frail strings for me must all be dumb,
  This melody will linger with thee yet,
  To whisper that thy child doth not forget,
  But that her spirit unto thine is near—
  In sympathy with every smile and tear.
  O mother, I am always with thee—why
  Should love like ours fear though the body die !

HAPPY, HAPPY FLOWERS.

Happy, happy flowers !
So smiling and so peaceful do you seem,
All bathed in sunlight and the crystal dew,
You do not know how sad it is to dream.

Happy, happy flowers !
Quaint Blue-bells, bluer than the summer sky,
And nodding 'mong the gently-swaying grass,
Whence are you—can you tell—and whence am I ?

Happy, happy flowers !
For you there is no sob within the sea,
You cannot hear the moaning of the wind ;
But ah ! it is far otherwise with me.

Happy, happy flowers !
You never knew the storms on life's rough stream,
But yet, I would not choose your even way,
Alas ! you know not what it is to dream !

SUMMER, WINTER, SPRING.

Swallow, swallow, soaring far,
As if seeking yonder star;
Singing joyfully thy song,
All those golden clouds among;
Rising swift from earth to sky,
Back again to earth to fly!

Swallow, ever on the wing,
Now no more we hear thee sing;
Birds and flowers—all, all are gone;
Winter finds me here alone:
"O that I like thee had wings!"
Thus forever my heart sings.

No more snow, but gentle rain:
" Swallow, art thou here again?
One day shall I too find wings!"
Thus forever my heart sings—
" And beyond that starry sky,
Shall I ever upward fly;
Far beyond or land or sea,
Where in dreams I've followed thee;
Far beyond the snow or rain,
Never to touch earth again!"

NIGHT.—A REVERY.

The shades of night have fallen now,
But clear and full shines out the moon,
And by its side there gleams a star,
Which, were I asked to give a name,
I'd call fair Hope. Calm summer eve!
The trees would seem to hold their breath,
Or softly sing their songs of peace.

O Nature! grand in all thy moods,
And answering to our human need:
Ofttimes so dark and wild thou art,
As if rude tempests shook thy frame;
Anon quite clear and calm again,
And stepping softly as a child!

Unfathomed are the minds of men,
Unspeakable their feelings deep;
We can but search and dimly know,
As if we peered through pale moonlight;
We darkly see, or not at all,
Like helpless children, crying, "where?"

DOUBT NOT.

Repel dark doubt,
Dismiss dread care,
Ah! wherefore should we fear,
When God is love,
And merciful,
And ever near?

The humblest life
That breathes on earth,
Lives through His law divine;
Let us not dream
His power can fail,
His wise design.

No atom's lost,
But ever change
Has worked throughout all time;
No end there seems—
Our brightest dreams
And most sublime

Can not discern
The Source of all,
Nor grasp His mighty plan ;
Each blade of grass
Receives His care—
Then, fear not, man !

No rankling doubt —
The spirit life
Will ever bloom in higher forms ;
So we may live
With present faith,
Above life's storms.

And hopeful hearts
More hopeful grow,
Though what shall be is dim ;
They look above,
And see His love,
And trust in Him.

SEA WEEDS.
(For Music.)

Alone with the sea—
Is there never a voice
    To return my heart's deep sigh !
    Alone with the sea—
And the moon and the stars
    That illumine yon lowering sky !

    Alone with the sea—
Can no one tell
    What the secret of her unrest !
    Alone with the sea—
I could throw myself
    And weep on her heaving breast !

    Alone with the sea—
I seem to hear
    In her moan my soul's own lay,
Like the cry of a child
That has lost it's home
    And asks but to know the way !

2

The tempest went from the ocean cave,
    And passed along the white sand ;
A gentle breeze awoke in the south,

And hastened across the land ;
And kissed the tear from the restless wave
And the sigh from the sounding deep,
And soothed with the softest lullaby
The ocean at last to sleep.

3

The stars are bright in the sky to-night,
   And the moon looks over the sea ;
But deeply impressed within my lone breast,
   Is a vision more lovely to me.

I hear the lave of the rippling wave,
   And a whisper from every tree ;
But over my soul doth a music roll,
   That is sweeter than all to me.

On the mountain low lie the clouds like snow,
   And a silence comes over the lea ;
But a holier calm like some heavenly balm,
   Is falling to-night upon me.

How beautiful now is the heaven's pure brow,
   And the glory on land and sea ;
But the moonlight stream of my fancy's dream,
   Is dearer than all to me !

QUESTIONINGS.

It haunts me everywhere I go,
By night or day, in joy or woe;
One great desire—the thirst to know.

To what end is my work to-day?
Or is it work, or is it play?
In vain I ask. What can I say?

Whereunto shall I set my aim?
I have not any wish for fame:
What profit is there in a name?

Sometimes methinks it cruel seems,
That Nature sendeth us no gleams—
Or only something vague as dreams—

Of what the future hath in store,
Of what life is at root and core;
And sadder evil I deplore,

That men unfettered dare not speak,
From their new fount of thought, but seek
To hide fresh truth from week to week;

Or wrestle with a ruthless fate,
Becoming martyrs soon or late:
Can faith not live on faith and wait?

Not idly wait; but, without fear,
Heroically making clear
Their trust in good—like Heaven-taught seer.

Is Nature slow? We cannot prove
Her works, alas! but only move
Within one little narrow groove.

We see the grass grow in the field;
The tree its lovely harvest yield;
But think! what kingdoms lie concealed!

The rushing torrent, roaring wind,
Are not more busy in their kind,
Than is the silent, brooding mind.

Self-poised, mysterious mind surveys
Material worlds, and counts their ways,
But of its own thought-life, the maze,

It only knows it knows not,—sighs
To feel assured that when it dies
It only changes and will rise,

And reassert its life, and power,
As stars return at midnight hour,
Or daisies come again to flower.

The germ of faith is in the soul;
Howe'er it be, we trust the Whole,
Nor fear,—whatever be the goal.

The power of one true master mind,
The power of many such combined,
Has it been—can it be—defined?

Man sends his thought from him afar,
Seas, mountains, fail its course to bar,
Shall he not speak from star to star?

What mystery escapes his lore,
That he may not one day explore,
While Doubt leads on from more to more?

Thou blessing Doubt, I welcome thee;
Sure symbol of activity:
We needs must question e'er we see.

'Tis doubt that teacheth us to wait,
That saves us from a hateful hate,
And opens to us Reason's Gate.

WEE WILLY.—A TRUE STORY.

As night comes creeping over day,
Elastic fancy soars away,
To take a glance through childhood's years,
All filled, as now, with joys and tears;
That "long ago," in fitful gleams,
Comes back to me like vivid dreams

The modest village church is there,
With well worn, ivy-mantled stair;
The spire that served to point the way
For many a traveller by day,
While superstition feared to mark
Its close proximity, if dark;
For thereabouts, the people said,
Wandered the spirits of the dead.

The village school-house I recall
More vividly, methinks, than all :
Of thirty pupils there was one—

A bright-eyed boy, brimful of fun—
A little boy, self-willed and strong,
And restless as the day was long.
What did he care for reprimand?
None did he fear in all the land;
Untamed as any forest bird,
He could not brook a wrathful word.

"Rebellious one!" the master thought,
"His rebel spirit shall be taught:
To him I'll show myself severe—
He shall obey or not be here!"

This was the way a war began
Between the pupil and the man;
From bad to worse the battle grew,
Nor man nor boy knew what to do.

Yet tender-hearted was the child,
With some quite tractable and mild.
I oft recall his large eyes yet,—
The forehead white, with veins so blue,

A thoughtful face, wherein there met
Both intellect and goodness too.

O that the master could have seen
What that young nature might have been—
Have known that, if strong will was there,
It needed all the greater care—
Have looked upon that will with pride,
Not striven to break it, but to guide!

"So good!" is sometimes said of one
Who lacks capacity for fun;
"So bad!" is oft applied to him
Who sees some sport in every whim:
Vocabulary misapplied—
The bad is oft the good belied!
The river from the highest source
Will onward roll with mighty force;
Untroubled, its swift waters clear
Will bear us blessings every year;
But rudely check its chosen path
(No surer way to rouse its wrath),

'Twill sweep with devastating train
O'er all the smiling fertile plain.

One morn wee Willie's vacant place
Reminded me of his wan face
The eve before. The weeks flew by—
He did not come—I wondered why.

A hasty messenger one day
Came seeking one called " little May,"
And told how darling Willy sent
Entreating that before he went
Away, his playmate would but come.
" Away!"—he meant to his long home!

With throbbing heart I quickly flew
To where he lay, but hardly knew
The wasted form and weakened voice.
Afraid to make the slightest noise,
In silence by his couch I stood,
While he in melancholy mood,
Drew down my face near to his own,

And whispered tremblingly and low,—
"Dear little May! Oh, must I go?"
The voice was but the faintest tone;
But still the restlessness was there,
Impulsive tenderness, most rare—
And then there came a single moan—
The eyes shone with angelic glow.

Naught could I speak; my heart was full:
"This, sturdy Willy of the school!"
All blinding came the bitter tears,—
No time to calm his anxious fears.
My poor wee Willy, pale and meek!
I made a pillow for his cheek
Against my own, and, as he smiled,
I kissed his brow, so white, so mild.
Some moments passed—a change appeared—
The change I waited for, yet feared:
The little sufferer had fled—
I held not Willy—he was dead!

The earthly body that he wore
   Was buried 'neath a willow tree,
And as I wept in sadness sore
   The willow seemed to weep with me.
Upon the little lonely grave
The branches would so gently wave,
And if a bird came nigh to sing,
Its note had aye a mournful ring.
The school-house children went that way,
But softly trod, or stopped their play.
Ofttimes, amid their sportive noise,
I listened for wee Willy's voice
(So hard is it to realize
In childhood, how a playmate dies!)
And if his tones I might not hear,
I still would dream his spirit near,
And smile to think, not far away,
He must be waiting "little May."

HYMN.

(By my Father. Reprinted from "Hymns and Anthems.")

Mysterious soul! thou wondrous power,
Not compassed by the passing hour;
But boundless, unconfined and free;
This earth is not a home for thee.

No orb's thy home; thou soar'st away
Beyond light's farthest piercing ray;
On through the boundless realms of space,
Immensity's thy dwelling-place!

Mysterious soul! Thy course sublime
Not fettered is by years of time;
Nor past nor future limits thee—
Thou livest in eternity!

Thou need'st no passport for the tomb,
No light to guide thee through its gloom;
For thou art life and light combined—
A ray of the Eternal mind!

PART THE SECOND.

TO THE NEW YEAR.

The wonder-land is nigh, though undescried,
   And worlds shall enter with the early dawn ;
   One moment, ere night's curtain be withdrawn,
   We pause to mark th' advancing human tide,
Which comes with steady flow; in joy and pride,
   Its burden bearing from the ages gone;
   Already building countless hopes upon
   That land it deems more fair than all beside.
Dark voiceless region, dreary, calm, and cold,
   Awaiting still man's advent on thy shore ;
   Thou giv'st him nought but what he brings to thee :
His faith and love go with him evermore—
   But yonder is the morn ! upon the wold,
   The New Year, smiling, steps from the "To Be !"

AH, ROSE SO SWEET!

Ah, Rose so sweet! the sweetest of all flowers;
   No sister hast thou to compare with thee;
   Rich, poor, and wise and simple, watch to see
   Thy early bloom, thou queen of summer bowers!
'Hush!' spake a pleading voice, 'no blossom towers
   Supreme o'er all her sisters of the lea;
   Associate are flowers by you and me
   With Time and Place,—from these derive their
                                  [powers.
The yellow Broom that decks my native shore
   And fragrant Heather on the mountain's brow,
   Forever must my truest favourites stand;
To me they're linked with all poetic lore,
   And memory dwells with pride upon them now,—
   Loved emblems of a wild, romantic land!'

MORNING.

The dawn had barely woke; the moon afar—
    A silver crescent on the lonely sky—
    Forsaken was by her vast company;
    But one alone remained—the morning star.
From out the east arose a crimson glow
    That, falling softly on the lake, awoke
    Not e'en the earliest singing-bird, nor broke
    The deep tranquillity of Time's dull flow.
Most solemn hush! "Is this the death of Night?"
    I said within my heart; "In Autumn-time
    The woods grow crimson weeping summer's flight,
While earth droops wearily and sighs forlorn."
    With wand-like touch, a flood of light sublime
    Dissolved the spell, and hailed the birth of Morn!

THE POET.

The Summer-bloom has left the garden now;
   And day has disappeared in night's dark cloud;
   The trees, so late with fruit and blossom proud,
   Before approaching Winter weep and bow.
Lo, how the poet walks with pensive brow
   Adown the forest, where the wind moans loud
   Among the withered leaves, which make a shroud
   For the dull earth, now naked in each bough!
How runs the lonely wanderer's silent muse?
   Does Nature's gloomy mantle rest on him?
   With sadness is his inspiration fraught?
Not so! his mind some gladness can infuse
   Into each hour, however dark or dim:
   The Poet's is th' ideal world of thought.

FRIENDSHIP.

One questions eagerly, "Can friendship die?"
   Another, as with warning, answers low:
   "The fickle winds of fortune ever blow,
   Full often severing the olden tie.
Mark how the soul of aspiration high
   Outstrips the lesser soul of progress slow;
   And say if time be not a ruthless foe
   Whom only rarest friendship can defy.
Unconsciously, perchance, may feeling wane;
   The turning-point will oft elude the mind,
   Which some day wonders how the coldness grew.
Behold yon rainbow through the glistening rain!
   Canst thou the limit of one colour find?
   Yet does the violet shade into the blue."

GEORGE ELIOT.

As when the siren voices held in thrall,
   In days of old, the wanderers by sea,
   Enchanting them with wondrous melody,
   So did thy spirit to our spirits call,
And keep them spell-bound in new realms of thought;
   And even as the song, divinely sweet,
   With undertone of sadness still is fraught,
   So, in thy voice did joy with woe compete.
Thyself, a shining light, thou knew'st the shade;
   But, from the silence of the soul's recess,
   The lamp of thy great genius shone afar:
The weary worker in his loneliness
   Descried the ray, and dreamed it could not fade.
   To him thou art as an immortal star!

[WRITTEN ON RETURNING FROM VISITING SOME HOMES OF THE POOR, OCTOBER 2, 1887.

TO THE ARTS.

Hail Music! Waft me now upon thy wing
   Beyond these vapours of the murky night;
   Bear me afar to regions fair and bright,
   Where with one grand accord the angels sing!
Thou whisperest of an ideal spring
   Where Poesy and all the Arts delight
   In honouring each; where the inspirèd sight
   Sees beauty underlying everything.
Ye white-robed seraphs—Music, Poesy—
   Descend amid earth's poverty and pain!
   Make sufferers forget their misery,
And evil-doers vow to sin no more;
   Say unto each: "My brother, try again!
   I would unlock for thee thy prison door."

TIME.

I heard a strange voice calling unto me;
   Did it not fall from yon etherial air,
   So wonderfully pure its tone and rare;
   Or was it breathed across the lonely sea?
Again the same voice sounded full and free:—
   "Time am I called; behold me everywhere;
   For destiny hath given to my care
   The Past, the Present, and the great To Be.
Go up unto the hill-top. I will show
   Myself to thee when busy day is done,
   And twilight shadows gather thick below;
For only to the great Infinite One
   Am I made visible in noon's pure glow:
   Man seëth me but in the setting sun."

IDEALS.

Not for the deed that's done is this our praise;
   Not to the word that's written bow we down;
   'Tis something greater far that we would crown:
   The highest work a higher thought can raise.
When life is painted in some noble phase,
   And skilful art has merited renown,
   The artist to himself will sadly own
   How feebly he his soul's clear thought conveys.
The picture's but a symbol from his hand,
   And symbolizes to *his* mind alone
   The fullness of his fancy's brightest gleam:
Admiring crowds will gaze—an endless band,
   And deem they follow out each thought and tone;
   But hardly one will catch the artist's dream.

FRIENDSHIP.

O Friendship! Do they deem thee but a name!
   Who calls thee so hath never seen thy face,
   Nor known the secret of thy winning grace—
   The love that cannot speak where it must blame.
Yet thou hast not been all unknown to fame:
   Among the records of the past we trace
   The story of Orestes, who for space
   Of years, 'mid trials sore, did never shame
The trust of Pylades—his chosen friend.
   Youth, fame, and love,—behold! how, without end,
   The throng still hurries on its anxious way!
There is but one of calm, unclouded brow,
   Whose beauteous crown shines with divinest ray.
   While Peace stands by—sweet Friendship, it is *thou!*

THOUGHT.

Serene is yon deep blue expanse above—
    Bright symbol of the tranquil human mind—
    The hurricane well passed; now calm, resigned,
    And shining with the universal love.
Low down upon that placid brow of heaven,
    A floating cloud, as if it sought a star,
    By music-loving summer winds up-driven,
    Appears—a white-winged thought blown from afar.
Transcendent thought! with thee in gloomy fears,
    We mourning sink into the vale of tears,
    Forsaking not the sorrow of thy night;
Or joyful follow in thy glorious lead,
    To wander with thee through the starry mead,
    Companions of thy glory, of thy light.

SONNET.

READ AT THE GOLDEN WEDDING OF E. N.

A word went forth upon the morning wind,
   Melodious falling on the dewy air,
   As pure as early snow-drop, and as fair—
   A benediction to our human kind.
Deep-sounding through the ages still we find
   Its wondrous consolation everywhere—
   A subtle charm for sorrow or dull care :
   By which the darkest clouds are silver-lined!
Thrice blessèd be the zephyr that has brought
   Such tidings from the far-off secret realm—
   A message linking earth to heaven above.
Our life-ship cannot wreck with this sweet thought—
   This gleaming talisman upon its helm,
   When sweet and low the morning wind says—Love.

SILENCE.

In silence do ye gather, shades of night!
    The sun in peaceful glory passed away;
    As quietly arises the new day;
    And gently fall the rays of the moon's light.
How doth the sparkling eye with glances bright
    Make revelation more than tongue can say—
    The inmost secrets of the heart betray!
    No speech is needed for the soul's insight.
To thought, O silence, thou'rt a very sun;
    Without thee, genius withers and grows pale,
    And fails to charm us with his fairest flower:
High-born art thou; even the great gods hail
    Communion with thee—consecrate thy hour.
    In silence nature's grandest work is done!

HOPE.

Tis she that walks before us day by day
    Who wooed us in our early infancy,
    In shining robes as fair, as fair could be,
    Enchanting us with an harmonious lay.
When later on we saw the alluring fay,
    Her voice resounded, if less merrily,
    With sweeter far and truer melody,
    While no less beautiful was her array.
HOPE leadeth still; her path and ours are one;
    No nearer her we come, no farther go;
    Old age is fain to grasp her pure, white hand;
For dimming eyes gaze wistfully—but lo!
    Just as our earthly pilgrimage is done,
    Her shadow falls upon the unknown land.

DESTINY.

In starry beauty falls the crystal flake,
    As if it caught from heaven's bright host the form,
    And, helplessly, upon the winter storm
    Is earthward swept—a brief abode to make.
O soul of heaven-born beauty! out of space
    And time, thou, too, dost drift unto the earth
    Awhile to dwell; and, fading, leave no trace,
    Unknowing aught or of thy end or birth.
Thy friends forsaking—though a chosen band;
    Alone departing—and perchance for aye;
    Ah, ruthless fate! What is thy stern command—
That henceforth each pursue a separate way?
    Or do the paths divide but to unite?
    E'en as the darkness alternates with light.

ON THE DEATH OF CARLYLE.

Dumb stands the world beside a new-made tomb;
  Unuttered even is the burial prayer;
  Yet not unhallowed is the silent air;
  A grief too deep for tears or prayers; a gloom
World-wide; for earth has seen her richest bloom
  Decay and pass into the vague 'somewhere'—
  That unknown sphere from which no traveller e'er
  Returned to tell humanity his doom.
O mighty heart! like to the changing sea
  To fury lashed, and back with sudden awe
  Subsiding (as if Eolus set free
The tempests, and, relenting, called them home),
  To thee—as once upon the Mount—a law
  Of Truth was given from yon celestial dome.

[WRITTEN WHILST STUDYING SPINOZA'S "ETHICS."]

From out the misty night of long-ago,
   A star arose upon the human sky,
   Unheralded by voice of prophecy,
   And passed away. And there was none to know.
But Time is just. The Present looks, and lo!
   Through the new power of its discerning eye,
   It sees a fuller day about us lie;
   The influence of that light's diviner glow.
May not the mind, illumined by that gleam,
   Its wealth of gifts behold in clear array,
   Tracing their promise for the years afar?
Awake humanity! No longer dream!
   Lose not the revelation of to-day!
   Spinoza was that new-light-giving star.

[FOUNDED ON A PERSIAN LEGEND.]

The child asks, " Is it true?" The story's old,
   Of a brave youth who all on good intent
   Alone about the world unwearied went
   For love of human kind, nor sought for gold.
His face was beautiful with thought ; his hold
   Of life but frail,—as if he had been meant
   For gentle ways, and could not have been sent
To battle with a world that bought and sold.
A wistful, far-off look grew in his eyes
   As if they said to all, "Goodnight, farewell !"
   Farewell it was.   In groves of paradise
A radiant maiden meets him.   " Who art thou?"
   He asks, " For none so fair on earth did dwell."—
   "*I am thy deeds,*" she says, "*that greet thee now !*"

LIFE'S PURPOSE.

"Life's purpose is accomplished!" exclaimed one,
   As, with a sigh, that was not all of pain
   Nor yet of pleasure all, he turned again,
   Repeating, "What I aimed to do is done!"
Then came another voice: "Your course is run!
   The longed-for goal no sooner we attain,
   Than we descry that fairer heights remain,
   And find at last our work is but begun.
The call becomes, 'So much remains to do!'
   Our feet have travelled but a little way,
   And we have lagged perhaps, and blundered too,
And wish we could forget—thankful that day
   Is still before us—that the flush of red
   Is not the evening glow, but dawn instead!"

"O Music! Art thou the evening breeze of this life,
or the morning air of the future one?"

Whence comes that melody? I sunward glance
    And see the hills in gold and amethyst,
    While off the earth there rolls a heavy mist:
    With fixèd gaze I stand as in a trance.
The glory deepens on the purple hills;
    The young moon looks down from her sea of blue;
    Anon the melody comes clear and true,
    And mingles with the voices of the rills.
Breathless, I watch the dying of the day;
    With hushed soul hearken to the heavenly sound;
    My heart is fluttering as if it would say,
"O music, who hath thee, a heaven hath found."
    Thou wakest in me some strange memory,
    Thou wanderer from that shore—Eternity.

THE POET'S DREAM.

Slight not the poet's thought. Like purest gem,
   He sees the truth shine deep in ocean's cave,
   And fain would reach to it if he might save
   The pearl, to place it in earth's diadem.
Slight not the poet's thought. From lofty sphere,
   The voice of love is calling unto him—
   A message from celestial seraphim,
   And fain is he that all the world should hear.
Slight not the poet's thought. He dreamed a dream
   Upon a cloud he sat, and saw below
Earth's chaos; and he cried, "Can sorrow cease?
Hast thou, O heaven, no healing to bestow?"
   An angel form appeared from a sunbeam,
   Saying, "Lo! Hope is here; Hope giveth peace."

THE IDEAL.

" What now is thine ideal ? " asks a friend,
    As with an earnest glance he turns to me ;
    " Each one hath his own vision ; let us see
    Wherein these differ, and whereto they tend.
Think of the world that is ; of what ' might be ' ;
    Of what was loveliest to you long ago—
    The shattered ideals—place them in a row—
    Beginning with the years of infancy."—
I strove then to call up the vanished past—
    A swift-drawn mental picture of the whole—
    Tracing each aim unto the present hour ;
But words were halting, and I could at last
    But say : " O sky-ward looking, fleet-winged soul !
    Earth hath no name for thine ideal flower."

OBLIVION.

Oblivion come ! Of this rough pilgrimage
  I weary am, and gladly would resign
  The world, and all that I had callèd mine.
  Yet could I wish that there might come an age—
An after-time—when, from vacuity
  (E'en as refreshed we waken from a sleep),
  I, strengthened, might arise, and vigil keep
  Once more with suffering humanity.
Of nature I can feel I am a part :
  Howe'er it be, we cannot separate,
  For we are surely one in mind and heart,
And no wave comes nigh her but touches me.
  The hand invisible that guides our fate,
  Shall still attend my sleep in Lethe's sea.

TO "OUR CLUB." OCTOBER, 1887.

The fire-lit room invites ; now is the hour ;
    Come friends, ye true and tried ones, gather round !
    The gloaming gray glides in without a sound—
    Gentle as starlight—with a soothing power.
For us the noisy crowd awhile be dumb ;
    And, following step by step our chosen theme,
    We'll build thought upon thought until our dream.
    Become the foreglimpse of a world to come !
Philosophy be our elected queen :
    Submissive to her voice our voices be ;
    Let doubt be frank before her without fear :
She cometh robed in soft humility ;
    Her glance is not less calm than it is keen,
    And nature's questions—all—to her are dear.

THE WANDERER'S DREAM.

Ere came the first sound of the matin bells,
    The angel we name Death, stood by my side :—
    " Fear not, child, tremble not if nigh I glide—
    But hearken how the joyful chorus swells!
The acclamation from high heaven tells
    That paradise unto some souls hath wide
    Its portals oped. How long thou may'st abide
    On earth—knows not the God that in thee dwells.
But this, lone pilgrim, I would have thee know—
    A message from th' Eternal Throne above—
    Thy friend I am alway, and not thy foe ;
On earth called Death, but in the heavens called Love.
    Long hast thou yearned to reach yon shining dome;
    Poor wanderer, take heart ! Behold thy home !"

THE FIRST SNOW.

The harvest now is o'er; the fields are bare;
   And yonder is the ploughman on the hill;
   The water freezes in the purling rill;
   Bleak desolation meets me everywhere.
Gray threatening sky; a frosty atmosphere;
   The haws o'er-ripe are falling from the trees;
   A fairy snowflake floating on the breeze,
   Announces that the Winter-king is near.
The withered leaves are moaning as I go,
   A requiem for the sweet season dead;
   Each little flower is hiding from the snow,
And happy swallows, ye hath southward fled!
   My spirit turns away: with other eyes,
   I still can see the genial summer skies.

OUR GUIDING STAR.

INSCRIBED TO " CRITIC."

Do we scan vainly this immense ' somewhere,'
   For hand to point the way that we should go,
   Or rule to guide us through this vale below,
   And listless sink at last in grim despair?
Ye constellations—worlds so far and fair
   Beaming in seeming joy—could ye but know
   The tragedy of life—its deeps of woe—
   In pity would ye leave your courses there!
Each for himself must find his own bright star;
   Each must discover the straight, upward path;
   Each one attain the life of truest beauty:
Haply we do not need to look afar;
   One word describes it, and that each one hath:
   Whate'er we have not, we have all our Duty.

"SO SAD, SO STRANGE, THE DAYS THAT ARE NO MORE!"

Aye, when the world seems all too drear and cold,
   And hopelessness stares me on every side,
   And melancholy only doth abide
   To wrap me in her heavy ebon fold,—
I can retire—disquietude untold—
   And unto her my troubles all confide,
   With her in waking dream sit side by side,
   And shed my tears as I was wont of old.
Her memory's a sanctuary now,
   Though long, long years have veiled her from my sight;
   Almost I feel her hand upon my brow,
And then the darkness is transformed to light;
   But when I cry, "My mother, it is thou!"
   The vision's gone: I sit alone with night.

PART THE THIRD.

MEDITATIONS FROM "DREAM-GROTTO."

"*And conscious life is King of Kings.*"

I

The quaintest grotto this! a hermit cell!
The passer-by discerns not the retreat;
No drop of rain to it can penetrate.
Here needs no toll of bell t'announce the hour;
The shadows write it on the smooth, green grass:
And yonder, on the horizon, Hesperus
Forgets not to proclaim the day is done.
The season is portrayed upon the trees;
On golden boughs the summer sighs 'farewell.'
A look of waiting falls upon the land—
As one may see the aged stand and gaze
Knowing the great deliverer is nigh.
Upon the shelving branches there are laid
Companion books: darkness conceals them now
(So little way the body's eye can see);
Yet one may reach to them with eyes of faith,
For soul subserves all earthly elements,
And mounts on them—the conscious King of Kings!

II

I watch the birds that hop about my feet
Across the lengthening shadows on the lawn,
And see them perch upon the slender twigs,
And lightly sway themselves from tree to tree,
Then soar into the peaceful blue of heaven,
And send to earth a perfect flood of song.

Oft will man envy these glad birds their wings,
Forgetting his soul's pinions, that can take
Him on from flower to flower and peak to peak
And upward to that vast ethereal dome
Beyond where bird can reach or wind may blow,
And back and forth through all the centuries
(From ages past to ages yet to be)
Until, as free as lark in yon blue sky,
He soars in the pure azure of his thought,
And utters songs that lift the human world.

III

Neath this hot sun, upon this summer day,
Earth grows alive; as if the glowing beams
Had floated life down from yon fiery orb,
Or summoned it from earth's deep sepulchre.
When our too slothful minds shall feel the sun
Of righteousness shine on them and grow warm
With right's enthusiasm, then shall we
Reflect that righteousness, and make the shade—
The darkest hours of life—shine beautiful
With chastened light—a moonlight of the mind!
Thou moonlight of the mind! In thy still air
The busy, garish day doth vanish quite;
Celestial melodies entrance the soul,
And thrill it with a joy not of the earth—
A rapture that doth hint of height on height—
A vast 'beyond'—an infinite foreground,
Warmed by the rays of an undying sun.

IV

Ah! whither, whither,—whither do we go?
Full sweetly from the hawthorn hedge the lark
Gave forth his plaintive note into the night—
A night that ever since hath darker been:
The crescent moon withdrew her promised light,
And not one little star remained in view.
By heaven and earth forsook, I was alone.

Beyond! Beyond! I think I hear ye say;
Or came the voice across the moaning deep?
Beyond! Ah, softly—ponder—beyond what?
What is 'beyond' in Nature's unity?

So all alone! such desolate despair!
A lone beginning to a lonelier end!
Each soul an isolated world: its life
Cut off at last as one might pluck a flower.
O mighty powers—ye gods! Are ye, too, lone?
Can ye feel pity? Can ye read the thought
Of beings far more lowly than yourselves?
Or, haply, do ye but make sport of them?
As men make sport with creatures less than they?

V

Among the maples and low-sighing pines,
Solemn I wander through the dusky gloom,
And think upon the loved forms of the past.
Where are they and how are they? Where am I?
Are they but farther on the thorny road
Which I am traversing? Do they await
Those whom they held the dearest here on earth?
Shall fond companions ever meet again?

So much I've pondered thus in this dark wood,
It now seems haunted by those spirit-friends.
The yellow leaves are dropping from each bough
Like symbols of our transitory life.
All change! But what a hope lies in the word!
When one is animated by the love of good,
Change can be naught but progress evermore.
Cherish this thought and hopelessness will die.

VI

Great book of Nature! In thee let us read,
And in thee lose this loneliness of soul,
Forgetting all for thine infinite truth—
As ills may sink in dark oblivion's sea,
While fancy roves afar in waking dreams.
Alone with Nature we are least alone.
Doth she not speak to us in undertones
Of murmuring water or of moaning wind,
And in the silent longings of the soul?
Let us not fear our thoughts; are they not Hers?
She is the Author and our Mother, She.

VII

See there the yellow butterfly that flits
From flower to flower with joy of its new life.
If it could look down on that chrysalis—
That lowly tent wherein it used to dwell,
And if its thought could wander farther back
To where it crawled a worm upon the dust,
How would it marvel at its painted wings,

And power to light upon the honied flower !
In all the fairy lore by fancy wove,
There's nothing to be found so strange as this ;
More wonderful is it to childlike mind,
Than when the lovely Galatea breathed.

    Whereto doth first the power of memory come ?
Man knows not of a past ; but shall he know ?
The hour that passes, shall he know it gone ?
Th' unknown—hath it not room for all his hopes ?

VIII

The mansion—is't the same I used to know ?
The colours seem too gaudy—no repose ;
The walls oppress—are prisonlike and cold :
No more the old familiar voices sound ;
The ivy's gone that twined about the tower ;
The wall-flower and the periwinkle, dead ;
E'en the old name will soon be quite forgot !

    Forgot ! aye, everlastingly forgot !
Unwitting pause we on that 'ever-more.'
Turn we the protean kaleidoscope,
Each revolution showing something new ;

One picture may not come before us twice,
Yet every image is therein contained;
Forms disappear—is it forever-more?
Howe'er it be, I hardly know this spot.
The change, perhaps, is mostly in myself;
I care not for the things I cared for once—
Or only care for them as relics old.
These volumes speak of superstition's sway;
The portraits—ancestors I never knew;
The quaint piano...'tis a curious toy;
To wander here, is living 'mong the dead.

Dead forms make the rich soil whence all life springs;
Our very hopes are nourished on decay.
Life-kindling thought is bearing us afar;
Our aspirations burst their barriers
(As surely as the lark breaks from her shell),
Soon as the fair ideal is matured.
Ye monuments of a dim past, farewell!
Through custom are ye all endeared to me;
Yet have I left you and that former self
Which once I was: we two are parted now;
Perforce each calls to each: farewell! farewell!

IX

Thou stately elm! Thy beauty speaks to me;
In thy life I can feel a lively joy;
Yet thou hast not the smallest part in mine!
Oft have I lingered 'neath thy sheltering arms;
Oft here found refuge from the burning sun,
And dreamed away the summer afternoon.
Far stretch the years before thee! Joyous groups
Will come to seek thy shade and carve their names
On thy great stem—as I have done erewhile.
Denied the power to think, thou art endowed
With strength of earthly life! while I, alas!
Endowed with thought, have shorter term to live.

Red grows the sky with wealth of light suffused—
Deep-orange red, and threatening, though still;
O'er-hanging clouds look solid as the hills,
And the low line of hills resembles clouds;
Night speedily her heavy mantle draws
O'er sea and land! 'tis blackness everywhere—
Except in the recesses of my soul:
There light is burning: there my real life—

A world of light though earth be wrapt in gloom—
A world in which thou, elm-tree, hast no share.

  O soul! the earth is but thy chrysalis;
Unhappy thou because thy tender wings
May not at once take the ideal flight.
Joy in thy growing pinions! Even now
They waft thee to that hidden world of thine,
Remote from earthly strife, and toil and pain,
Where—like the acorn springing underground—
The spirit grows in its vast solitude,
One day to rise to its ideal home.

  As water mounteth to its source's height,
So mounts the soul unto its highest thought.
What is the spirit's source but the Supreme!
Then to the All Holy doth the soul aspire.
Ponder this well, and death itself must die.

X

All, all is still! The meadow, hill, and wood;
The cattle sleeping on the new-mown hay;
The water motionless upon the lake;

The moon enthroned high on the midnight sky;—
All, all, is rest, yet life and harmony.

Why rest not I? If I could only fold
This restless brain, like petals of that flower!
If I could lay down *me* in shade retired,
Where winds would lull me to a dreamless sleep,
My brain commanding thus, "Go, take thy rest!"

As we mount higher up the scale of life,
The less of rest doth there appear to be;
For though great Nature seem awhile to pause,
And silence fill the cavern of the night,
And though the clouds lie mute like sleeping gods,
Life conscious is, and there's no rest at all.
No rest at all—or only perfect rest—
That grand repose where rest and work are one!
The rest, that is, when o'er earth's canopy
The northern lights keep at their ceaseless play;
The rest that is, when hid from human eye
The acorn prophesies the coming spring;
The rest that is, when wearied hands lie still
While thought communeth with the One Supreme!

All, all is still. The day is hid in night;
But soon the night will hide within the day;
And noiseless glides the chariot of the morn.
All, all is still. This hour be consecrate.
My spirit, onward! self-controlled—self-poised!
Till this unceasing, everlasting change,
Become to thee—as to the Eternal—rest!

PART THE FOURTH.

"There are so many tender and holy emotions flying about in our inward world, which, like angels, can never assume the body of an outward act, so many rich and lovely flowers spring up which bear no seed, that it is a happiness that poetry was invented, which receives into its limbus all these incorporeal spirits, and the perfume of all these flowers."

JEAN PAUL RICHTER.

POET AND READER.

(From the German of Stöber.)

Wouldest thou a poet be?
   Calm be thought, as if for prayer;
That thy spirit reverently
   Enter beauty's temple fair.
That thou see her features clear,
   All with pensiveness o'erlaid;
Till before thee she appear
   Fully, as of marble made.

Wouldest thou a poem read?
   Calm be thought, as if for prayer,
That before thy soul may speed,
   Image of the poet, rare.
That, through his own being, thou
   May'st descry his path with awe,
And, through his pure vision, now
   See the ideal that he saw.

BARCAROLLE.

(From the French of Théophile Gautier.)

Come, whither wilt thou sail?
  My pretty maiden, tell;
For favouring is the gale,
  See'st thou the canvas swell!

The rudder is of gold,
The sail a silken fold,
  And ivory the side;
An orange is the freight,
An angel's wing the gate,
  A seraph is the guide.

Come, whither wilt thou sail?
  My pretty maiden tell;
For favouring is the gale,
  See'st thou the canvas swell!

The Baltic shall it be?
Or coast of Normandy?
   Or island of Java?
To Norway would you go?
And see the snow-flower blow?
   Or blossom d'Angsoka?

Come, whither wilt thou sail?
   My pretty maiden, tell;
For favouring is the gale,
   See'st thou the canvas swell!

Conduct me, said the fair,
To that inspiring air,
   Where love is love for aye.—
That land, my gentle child,
Remote from this rude wild,
   Think you to reach to-day?

THE LETTER.

(From the German of Heine.)

The letter thou hast sent me,
    Shall not me anxious make;
To say thou dost repent thee,
    Should not twelve pages take!

Twelve pages of close writing—
    A manuscript—to tell,
That what thou art inditing
    Doth truly mean—farewell!

THE SERENADE.

(From the German of Uhland.)

What doth from slumber waken me?
    Sweet music do I hear;
O mother, see! who may it be
    So late at midnight drear?

"I nothing hear, I nothing see,
   Ah! slumber on, my boy!
A serenade they sing to thee,
   To bring thee dreams of joy!"

Not earthly music do I hear;
   It brings both joy and light;
The angels call me soft and clear—
   O mother dear, Good-night

COULD I BUT GO!

(From the French of Sully-Prudhomme.)

Could I but go to him and say:
"She now is yours—and, from this day,
   In my life hath not any part:
Ungrateful she hath been of late—
But she is pale and delicate
   In pity take her to thy heart!

Hear me then without jealousy,
For the wing of her fantasy
    Hath all too surely passed me by:
Of her disdain much could I tell—
But, where she loves, she loveth well;
    Oh! keep the tear-drop from her eye!"

If I could go to him and say:—
"Almost too sad her pensive way;
    Offer to her some flower each morn—
The softest blue rather than rose;
These daily courtesies disclose
    Thy love— a love she did not scorn."

Then I could an assurance feel,
That she is cherished for her weal—
    Though not by me—yet as I would—
Too cruel one! forsaking me;
My torture thou shalt never see.
    I cannot go—but if I could!

(From the German of Justinus Kerner.)

My picture* this? I cannot trace
   Herein the likeness to my face;
Well-taken doth the coat appear;
   The attitude,—the stick is here!

THAMIRE TO THE ROSES.

(From the German of J. N. Götz..)

My beloved, when we parted,
   Vowed that ere your buds had blown
He would come; but broken-hearted,
   Roses, see me still alone!

**Cytherea's daughter, fairest
   Rosebud! spare, ah spare me pain
For his promise if thou carest,
   Close again, ah close again!

---

* On receiving a portrait of himself done by his sister.

** Cythere was a Greek name of Aphrodite or Venus.

POETRY.

(From the German of Justinus Kerner.)

Poetry is a deep pain,
   And it comes—the real song,
Only in dark sorrow's train,
   Gliding through the heart along.

Greatest poems are, alas!
   Speechless, like to greatest pain;
Through the broken heart they pass
   Mute, like shadows on the plain.

ON THE DEATH OF A CHILD.

(UHLAND.)

He came and went, and left small trace—
A flying guest to this strange land;
   The 'Whence?' and 'Where?' we only know:—
From out God's hand back to His hand.

OH SAY, SWEET LITTLE BIRD OF MINE.

(From the German of Hebbel.)

"O say, sweet little bird of mine,
  O say, what distant goal is thine?"
      I cannot say,
      Yet must away,
The path I surely can divine!

"O tell, sweet little bird, to me,
What hope hath promised unto thee?"
      Soft air to greet,
      With odour sweet,
And a new Spring beyond the sea!

"That country far, thou hast not seen;
  Perchance it is not, nor hath been?"
      All that you ask,
      Were a hard task,
For me to answer you, I ween!

The bird flew o'er the desert sand,
   No guide had it from human hand;
      A day more fair,
      And balmy air,
   Have welcomed it in a far land.

THOU AND I.

(From the German of Hebbel.)

We dream of one another,
   And from our dreams awake
To live and love together,
   Each for the other's sake.

Forth from my dream thou goest,
   As I go forth from thine;
We die in self-forgetting—
   Resigning 'mine' and 'thine.'

Upon a Lily tremble
   Two drops so pure and round;
They mingle, calmly flowing
   Together to the ground.

HEART OF MINE.

(From Heine.)

Heart of mine, thou longest ever,
   For the olden happy time,
When the days were spent in pleasure,
   Simple, innocent, sublime!

Now 'tis hurry never ceasing,
   Envy, poverty and woe :
God is dead ; confusion reigneth
   Everywhere on earth below.

Darkness o'er the world is brooding,
   Rottenness is at the core :
Were it not for thee, my darling,
   I would give the struggle o'er!

IDEALS.

(From the German of Scherer.)

Comes a high-born thought this hour,
    Let it from you never,
Till you have it in your power
    Ever and forever.

If on duty's path you go,
    And a sorrow press you,
Close with it as with a foe,
    Fight it till it bless you.

BY THE SHORE.

(From the German of R. Gottschalk.)

What write the billows on the sand?—
    They can but tell their bitter pain,
    That they but come to go again—
So short a sojourn on the land!

I gaze upon the sea to-day.
    My sweetest joy and dearest hope,
I've written on the sandy slope:
    The waves are washing it away.

TO THE WIND.

(From the German of Lenau.)

I wandered to a foreign land,
    But ere I went I looked around;
    Her lips moved, and I heard a sound,
And then she waved her little hand.

I know it was some loving word
    She sent to cheer me on my way;
    But what it was I could not say;
The heartless wind alone had heard.

That I must leave my only bliss,
    Was not enough, too cruel wind!
    But thou must steal her message kind!
But thou must snatch her parting kiss!

RESIGNATION.

(From the German of Fr. von Sallet.)

Although they take from me my sight,
    They cannot thus obscure the sun;
In dungeon though I lie to-night,
    Yet Freedom's battle shall be won.

Although they bind my ready hand,
    Because it used the pen for sword,
Nor pen nor sword shall fail the land,
    While live true hearts that fear the Lord.

Although my voice be stifled quite,
    The breath omnipotent is here;
Th' immortal tone—the Infinite—
    Shall fill a million voices clear.

Think not the spring-time over yet
    With its abundant life and light,
Because some evil hearts have met,
    To kill a Nightingale at night.

THE WAKENED ROSE.

(*From the German of Fr. von Sallet.*)

The Rose-bud dreamed of warm sunshine,
Of rustling leaves and eglantine,
Of the melodious waterfall,
And of the nightingale's sweet call,
Of how caressing zephyrs blow,
And of the fragrant valleys low.

The bud awoke a full-blown Rose,
And through its tears a smile now glows,
For it can hear and it can see
The earth and air hold jubilee.
Its dream is realized, and lo!
With joy, and trembling more and more,
In its its surprise it whispers slow:
I think—I must have lived before!

APRIL.

(From the German of Geibel.)

Thou balmy April evening,
    I love thy beauty rare ;
The clouds obscure the heavens,
    A star shines here and there.

The breath of love is filling
    The zephyrs as they blow ;
The fragrance of the violet
    Is wafted from below.

O for a strain of music
    To suit the pensive hour—
Some cadence low and tender
    To tell its soothing power !

GOOD-NIGHT.

(*From Theodor Körner.*)

    Good-night !
Rest ye weary from your pain.
Silently the day is dying,
Ended now your care and sighing
Till the morning break again.
    Good-night !

    Rest awhile !
Let the weary eyelids close !
Over all a stillness falleth—
Hearken, 'tis the watchman calleth !
Night hath solace for our woes.
    Rest awhile !

    Slumber now !
Dream a dream of happy meeting !
Thou who art by love forsaken,
Shalt in fancy re-awaken
To the dearly loved one's greeting.
    Slumber now !

> Good-night !
> Slumber till the break of dawn ;
> Slumber till you hear the warning
> Whispered by the breath of morning.
> God is watching ; slumber on !
> Good-night !

THOU EVERYWHERE.

(From the German of Schultze.)

When the evening glow is dying,
Rise the moon and stars on high ;
When the stars and moon are fading,
Steps the sun into the sky.

In the heavens' crimson glory,
In the sun's illuming glance,
In the moon and all the planets,
See I but thy countenance.

Other forms may pass before me,
None I seem to heed but thine,
From afar I feel thy coming,
As if thy thought called to mine.

Yet when thou art by me sitting—
Then, indeed, I nothing see,
For my eyes o'erflow with weeping,
Joy and pain come over me.

Ah, I wish not to forget thee,
Cruel though the memory be,
Ever art thou near my spirit,
Though forever far from me.

SPRING SONG.

(From Heine.)

Softly thro' my listening soul
Sweetest chimes are sounding ;
Little spring-song onward roll,
Far and wide resounding.

Pause not till thou reach the cot
Where the Violet's springing ;
Whisper to the Rose my heart
Greets her in thy singing.

THE COT.

(From the German of Gleim.)

A modest little cot have I,
That just across the mead doth lie ;
A little brooklet purleth near,
Whose water floweth crystal clear.

My little cot you scarce may see
For yonder stately bending tree,
Which seems to look with kindly care
Upon the lonely dweller there.

And now a little nightingale
Is sweetly singing in the vale ;
So clear his note that one must stay
And hearken to him by the way.

Thou little maid with soft brown hair,
Who long hast been my joy and care,
I go, the storm-wind bloweth free :
Wilt thou not seek the cot with me ?

A POEM, THOU.

(From the German of Feodor Löwe.)

A rare and quite mysterious book,
   Is thy dear face to me ;
On whichsoever side I glance,
   A poem I can see.

But when therein I fain would read,
   And all my thoughts engage,
The roguish look within thine eye,
   Will slyly turn the page.

THE CASTLE BY THE SEA.

(From the German of Uhland.)

Hast seen yon castle standing
  Beside the crystal sea,
Around its tower commanding
  The white clouds wandering free:

Hast seen it downward bending
  To kiss the water clear,
Its summit high ascending
  To touch the heavenly sphere?

"Ah yes, I know its seeming—
  That castle by the sea—
The moon above it gleaming,
  The mist about the lea."

Did breeze and crested billow
  Sound loudly forth and long,
And from the festive chambers
  Came there a mirthful song?

" The wind and e'en the ocean
    But uttered plaintive sighs,
A wail of deep emotion
    Called tears into my eyes."

O did'st thou see the waving
    Of the monarch's crimson gown,
The precious jewelled setting
    Of the fair queen's golden crown ;

A maiden were they leading
    With rapture and with grace,
Celestial glory beaming
    Upon her lovely face ?

" The regal pair were sitting
    Without a chaplet rare,
In mourning robes and fitting :
    The maiden was not there."

PRIERE.

(From the French of Sully-Prudhomme.)

Ah, if you knew how I deplore
My solitude continually,
Sometimes before my cottage door
    You would pass by.

If you but knew the joy I took
In meeting but your fleeting glance,
Up to my window you would look
    As 'twere by chance.

If you but knew what comfort sweet
My heart has known when near you stood,
You could not hesitate to meet—
    No sister would,

If you but knew what I could tell!—
My *love*, and if you knew the how,
I almost think, perhaps,—that—well—
    You'd enter now.

MY HEART, I WISH TO ASK THEE.

(From the German of Fr. Halm.)

My heart, I wish to ask thee,
    What then is love, O say?
"Two souls with one thought only,
    Two hearts tuned to one lay!"

And say, whence cometh love then?
    "We know not of the where!"
And say, how goeth love then?
    "What goes was never there!"

And tell me, what is pure love?
    "For self it hath no will!"
And when is love the deepest?
    "When it is calm and still!"

And when is love the richest?
    "That is it when it gives!"
"And O, how talketh love, then?"
    "It doth not talk—it lives!"

CHAINS.

(From the French of Sully-Prudhomme.)

All have I wished to love, and now unhappy am,
    For of misfortunes I have multiplied the cause;
Innumerable ties have broken my sweet calm;
    The world with all its objects are to me as laws.

At once all things attract, and with an equal force;
    The truth with its own light; th' unknown with luring tones;
A golden ray hath linked my heart unto its Source;
    The stars with silken threads have bound me to their zones.

Soft melody is flowing to me like a tide;
    The odour of the rose awakens a new bliss;
And smiles can say to me, come hither and abide!
    While on my lips there lives the freshness of a kiss.

My life is hanging on such perishable thread;
    To beings that I love I'm like a captive elf;
The slightest breath of care that unto them is wed,
    Can rob me always of a portion of myself.

TO-MORROW.

(From the French of Victor Hugo.)

The future ours? Ah, no!
   It is the Gods' alone!
The hours are ringing low
   "Farewell" in every tone.
The future! Think! Beware!
   Our earthly treasures rare—
Hard-won through toil and care—
   Our palaces and lands,
Great victories, and all
   Possessions, large and small,—
But only to us fall,
   As birds light on the sands!

[Translation.]

A beauteous face illumed the way to Heaven:
    No more on earth is aught that can delight me;
    To souls elect, uprising, I unite me—
    A grace to mortal man but rarely given.
So well the work accords with Him who made it,
    That unto Him it lifts me: my life's story
    Is formed of thought and deed to suit its glory:
    It did command me: I have but obeyed it.
And if from these two eyes so brightly shining
    I turn not, but do recognize their fitness
    To guide me still upon the path supernal;
Enkindled at their fire, myself resigning,
    I shall reflect their lustre; and bear witness
    To joy, that reigneth in the Heavens, eternal.

ITALIAN SONNET.

BY MICHAEL ANGELO.

La forza d'un bel volto al ciel mi spiona
   (Ch' altro in terra non è che mi diletti),
   E vivo ascendo tra gli spiriti eletti;
   Grazia ch'ad uom mortal raro si dona.
Sì ben col suo Fattor l'opra consuona
   Ch'a Lui mi levo per divin concetti;
   E quivi informo i pensier tutti e i detti;
   Ardendo, am ando per gentil persona.
Onde, se mai da due begli occhi il guardo
   Torcer non so, conosco in lor la luce
   Che mi mostra la via, ch'a Dio mi guide;
E se nel lume loro acceso io ardo,
   Nel nobil foco mio dolce riluce
   La gioja che nel cielo eterna ride.

PART THE FIFTH.

GERMAN LOVE.

Found among the papers of a stranger. Edited and accompanied with a preface by *Max Müller.*

(*Translated from the German.*)*

I.

PREFACE.

WHO has not some time in his life sat down to a writing table where but shortly before sat another, who now rests in the grave? Who has not opened the drawers that for long years concealed the secrets of a heart that now lies hidden away in the hallowed peace of the churchyard? Here lie the letters which to him, the dear one, were so dear. Here are the pictures! here the books, with marks on every page. Who can explain them? Who can gather the scattered petals of a faded rose, and restore to them their first fragrance! The flames, that among the Greeks received the bodies of the deceased, as well as such things as these had treasured, are still the safest receptacle for the relics of the departed. With the most delicate hesitation does the bereaved friend turn over the pages which no living eye hath seen, and, having convinced himself that they contain

*Published by approval of Prof. Max Müller.

nothing intended for the public gaze, he throws them upon the glowing coals. They ignite, and are gone!

From such flames the following few pages have been saved. They were intended at first for friends only, but now they are permitted to wander away among strangers. How gladly would the editor have given more of those "recollections!" Unfortunately many of the pages were so far destroyed that it was found impossible to put them together again.

MAX MÜLLER.

OXFORD, January, 1866.

FIRST RECOLLECTION.

Childhood has its mysteries, but who can describe them? We have all wandered through that silent wonder-land. We have all once opened our eyes in happy bewilderment, and the beautiful reality of life has dawned upon our souls. Who we were, or where we were, we knew not; the whole world was ours, and we belonged to the whole world. Life was without beginning and without end—without stagnation and without pain. Our hearts were glad as a spring sky, fresh as the scented violet, calm as a Sunday morning.

How is the peace of childhood disturbed? How is it that we are driven out of this untroubled existence to find ourselves suddenly alone and lonely, grappling with the problems of actual life?

Answer not with stern brow that "sin" is the cause; say, rather, "We do not know; we can only submit." Is it sin for a plant to blossom, and bear fruit, and fade, and turn to dust? Is it sin that changes the caterpillar to a cocoon, and the cocoon to a butterfly, and the butterfly to dust? Is it sin for a child to grow to manhood, and age, and turn to dust? What is "dust"?

Choose to answer, "We do not know; we can only submit."

But ah! how sweet it is to think back on the springtime of life—to remember! In the hot summer, the sad autumn, the cold winter, there comes now and then a spring-like day, when the heart says, "I feel just as though it were spring!" To-day is such a one, and so I throw myself down on the soft moss in the fragrant wood, and stretch out my weary limbs, and look up through the green foliage to the infinite blue, and think, "How did it all seem when I wås a child?"

The beginning! If only there were no beginning! For with the beginning remembrance suddenly stops. And if we meditate upon childhood, and before that, and before that again, the mystic beginning is ever receding and receding; just as if a child sought to place its hand on the spot where the blue heaven rests on the brown earth, and runs and runs and grows weary, finding that the blue sky is just as far off as ever.

Yet a beginning of some sort must have been. What, then, do we all know about it? Memory gives itself a shake, like a poodle that has just emerged from a pond. When it has time to get the water out of its eyes, it looks up with a sort of surprised air, as much as to say, "Here I am after all!"

But I do believe I remember the first time I saw the stars. It may be that I had seen them often before, but there was one evening that something went on within me which made my little "I" more observant than usual. I was filled with fear somehow, and I sat in my mother's lap, and the cold made me shiver. My mother pointed to the bright stars, and I looked and wondered, and thought how shining and pretty she had made them!

All that first period seems filled with the loving face of my mother, the solemn glance of my father, a garden, a summer-house, soft, green grass, a curious old picture book, a venerable church from which came the sound of an organ whose tones made me feel, oh, so happy!

Then there comes a time when everything becomes more distinct. Not only are there mother and father, but sisters and brothers and friends and teachers,—and a crowd of strangers.

Oh, yes! of these strangers how much is engraven upon my memory!

SECOND RECOLLECTION.

Not far from our house stood a large building with many towers. The house had many windows, and these were hung with crimson silk and gold tassels. All round the court-yard stood linden trees, and the turf was strewed with their fragrant, white blossoms. Often I had looked in there, and in the evenings when the linden perfume was so sweet, and the windows lighted, and I saw forms moving here and there like shadows, and the music sounded, and carriages came driving along and ladies and gentlemen alighted aud hurried up the steps, I could not help asking myself " Why do you not go in too?"

One day my father took me by the hand, and said "Come, we will go to the palace. You must behave very nicely, and should the Princess speak to you, you must kiss her hand." I was about six years old, and rejoiced as one only can rejoice at that age. I had so often thought about the moving shadows that were visible in the evening when the rooms were lighted, and had heard so much said of the goodness of the

Prince and Princess—how much they did for the poor and suffering, that it seemed to my childish fancy that I knew all about what went on at the castle, and I felt as intimately acquainted with the Prince and Princess as I did with my leaden soldiers.

Yet my heart beat fast as I went up the steps with my father. Whilst he was telling me that I must say—"Your Highness," to the Prince, and "Your Serene Highness" to the Princess—the folding doors opened, and I saw a tall figure with clear, glancing eyes approaching. Then the beautiful lady smiled as she held out her hand to me. I could not longer restrain myself. Whilst my father stood at the door making a profound bow, I ran towards the lady, threw my arms round her neck, and hugged her as if she had been my mother. The Princess did not seem displeased, but stroked my hair and laughed. My father, however, drew me away, saying "that I had been very rude, and that he would never bring me there again." The blood flew to my cheeks, and I felt that my father did me an injustice. I looked round at the ladies and gentlemen assembled, expecting that they would take my part, but they were all laughing. The tears filled my eyes, and I ran away out of the door, down the steps, past the long row of lindens, and at last reached my mother, and threw myself into her arms.

"Why may I not love people who look at me with such kindly eyes?" I sobbed out.

"You may love them, but you must not show it," said my mother, soothingly.

"And why not show it—is it wrong?" I went on.

"No, no, my son; you are right; but when you are older you will understand that you cannot embrace everybody that looks kind and good."

That was a sad day. My father came home and insisted that I had been naughty. In the evening I said my prayers to my mother and went to bed. But I could not sleep. The question "What are 'strangers' that we dare not love them?" kept me tearful that I could not sleep.

Poor human heart! Even thy spring-tide leaves get nipped by the rude elements. We are taught to stand, to walk, to speak and to read; but nobody teaches us to love. Yet love, 'tis said, is the ground of our being. As the heavenly bodies attract each other, and are held in their places by the eternal law of gravity; so do heavenly souls attract each other, and are held by the eternal law of love. A plant will not blossom without sunshine, nor does the human plant thrive without love. And the love of the child is of that immeasurable kind that no plummet fathoms—a love that knows nothing of more or less, but that goes out to the object with the whole power of its being.

How little, alas! of this love remains ere we have completed the first half of life's circle! The child has learnt that there are 'strangers,' and therefore ceases to be a child. The spring of love is hidden. We walk through the din of the streets with weary-like, expressionless faces. Hardly do we risk a greeting as we pass each other by, for we have experienced what it is to meet with no response, and the wounds are still tender. At length the petals of the soul's blossom are nearly all bruised or blighted; in the inexhaustible well of love but a few drops remain with which to cool our tongues that we may not quite faint. These drops we still call love. But that is no longer the pure, full, glad love of the child. It is a love made up of anxiety and pain—a love which quickly passes away, like rain upon hot sand. It is love which exacts, not love which gives—love which asks, "Wilt thou be mine?" not love which says "I must be thine!" It is egotistical, despairing love. And that is the love of most youths. It blazes up and leaves nothing but smoke and ashes. Perhaps we have all once labored under the delusion that these poor rockets were rays of an eternal love!

When all about us becomes dark, and we feel alone; when all men go by us upon our right hand and upon our left, and none know us; then there arises in our hearts a feeling—we know not what to name it, for it is neither love nor friendship. One would like to call to each passer-by, "Do you not know me?" At that moment a man feels that there is a tie of *man* to *man* that is closer than that of brother to brother, father to son, friend to friend, and an old saying rises to our lips, "'Strangers' are neighbors." Why, then, pass them coldly by?

Again our answer, "We do not know; we must submit."

Two trains whiz past each other. A passenger on one exchanges a glance with a passenger on the other. "Oh, that we could have shaken hands!" is a feeling that rises in the soul of each. But each is driven in an opposite direction, farther and farther apart.

An old philosopher says, "I saw the débris of a shipwreck floating on the sea. Only a few splinters met, and these held but a short time together. A storm arose and drove them east and west. The same thing is happening among men. The great shipwreck itself nobody has seen!"

THIRD RECOLLECTION.

Clouds are of but short duration on the sky of childhood; a shower of tears, and they have disappeared. Very soon I was at the castle again. The Princess gave me her hand, which I kissed, and then she brought in the young princes and princesses, and they and I played together as if we had been acquainted for years. These were happy days. When I returned from school—for now I went to school—I walked over to the castle. There, there was everything that the heart could desire. All that belonged to the young Princes belonged to me, or so I thought. I could take the playthings home, if I liked, and keep them; often I gave them away to poor children. I was a communist in the full sense of the word. It was a long time before I could understand the difference between *meum et tuum*—the one seemed to me to shade into the other.

At this period, when I went to the castle not only to play, but to learn French, another form rises in my memory—the daughter of the Prince, the Countess Mary. Her mother had died at her birth, and the Prince had married again. When first I saw the Countess Mary I cannot exactly tell. Gradually she steps out of the darkness of early memory, until she stands before me like a moon that in the midst of a stormy night has suddenly the veil of cloud drawn off her face. She was always languid and silent, and I had never seen her otherwise than stretched out upon the couch on which she was carried into the room by two servants. She lay in long, soft, white robes, her hands folded, here face pale and calm and lovely. Often, as I looked at her, I became lost in thought, and asked myself if it were possible that she also could be a "stranger." Then she would lay her hand upon my head, and I felt that I could say nothing, but only gaze into her lustrous eyes. On days when she was stronger than usual she would sit up on her couch, and then it seemed as if the rosy hue of the sunrise overspread her countenance, and she talked with us, and amused us with delightful stories. I do not know how old she was. Though childilke in her helplessness, her mind seemed matured in its earnestness and calmness. Why, with all her beauty and frailty, she had been sent upon this earth, when she might have rested so peacefully with the angels, and been borne along upon their white wings, I could not understand. How I wished that I could have borne part of her burden. I could have prayed from my innermost heart that she might have been relieved from her sufferings.

One warm day in spring she was carried into our playroom. Perfectly white she looked, and her eyes more brilliant than ever. Sitting up on her couch, she called us round her. "To-day is my birthday," she began, " and I was baptized in spring. It is possible that I may soon be called away," she continued, looking smilingly at her father, "though I could wish to remain here. When I am gone I do not wish to be forgotten, and so I have brought a ring for each of you." She then kissed her brothers and sisters, and gave to each of them a ring. One ring remained upon her finger. She lay back as if exhausted. My eyes met hers, and as the eyes of a child speak clearly, she must have read what was going on in me. I would much rather not have had the last ring, feeling that I was a "stranger," and could not be dear to her as her brothers and sisters. A pang shot suddenly through my breast, as if an adder had stung me, and I did not know how to conceal my agony. She laid her hand upon my head, and looked down into my eyes, so that I felt that I had not a thought that was not plain to her. Drawing the last ring from her finger, she gave it to me, saying, "That one I meant to take with me when I parted from you; but it is better that you wear it. You have an impetuous and tender heart; may it be guided, not hardened." She then gave me the ring, and kissed me as she had done her sisters and brothers. I cannot describe what I felt. I loved her as a boy may—with a singleness of heart that is not often found in manhood. But I reflected that she belonged to the "strangers," to whom it was not permitted to show one's feelings. The earnest words she had spoken I did not fully comprehend. I only knew that her soul stood very near to mine—as near as two human souls could be. All bitterness had left me. I felt no more alone, no more excluded from her circle. Then I thought it had been a sacrifice on her part to give me the ring, and I said with a trembling voice, "Thou must keep the ring, if it be thy wish to give it to me; for what is thine is mine." She looked at me with wonder. Then she took the ring, and put it on her finger, and kissed my forehead, saying in a low voice, "Thou dost not know what thou sayest. Learn to understand thyself, and thou shalt be happy, and make others happy."

FOURTH RECOLLECTION.

Each life has its years during which one goes forward as on a level, monotonous road, almost unconsciously, or only with a sad consciousness of having got over some distance—of having become older. So long as the river of life flows smoothly, it always seems the same water, and only the landscape appears to vary. But then come the cataracts of life. These take hold of the memory, and even when we have left them behind and are fast drawing to the silent ocean of eternity, we still hear in the distance their rush and tumble, and feel, somehow, that the strength that remains to us and impels us forward, has its source in these cataracts.

School-time was past, and the early, merry days of university life were past, and many fair dreams of life were past. But one thing remained—faith in God and man. Life was quite other from what my little brain had fondly dreamed, but on that very account had it taken on a higher meaning. The presence of an incomprehensible was the proof of a godly in the earthly. "Nothing can happen to thee but as God wills," was the philosophy of life as I gathered it.

When the summer vacation arrived I returned to my native city. To meet again! what a joy that is! No one has ever explained it, but "seeing again," "finding again," "recollection," is the secret of almost all our happiness. Whatever one sees or hears for the first time may be beautiful or grand, but it is too new, and therefore surprises us, and the sense of repose is wanting; the effort after enjoyment is greater than the enjoyment itself. In returning to one's native city after a lapse of many years, the soul floats unconsciously in a sea of recollections, and the dancing waves bear it, as in a dream, along the shores of the days that are no more. There a house has been pulled down, and a new one built; that was the house where our old music-master lived. He is dead. What a delight it was once to pause and listen under his window! How would the great, sensitive soul, the drudgery of the day over, improvise for his own refreshment, and like a steam-engine letting off superfluous steam, give vent to his pent-up emotion!

Then comes one recollection after another, until the

waves of thought meet, and a deep sigh escapes us, reminding us that we have been lost in a waking dream, and had forgotten to breathe. Then our dream-world vanishes, like a ghost of the night before the crowing of the cock.

What changes at the palace! The Princess was dead; the Prince had retired to Italy. The eldest Prince, with whom I grew up, had become Regent. Many a year had elapsed since I had ascended the steps of the palace, and yet there lived there a being whom I named almost daily, and the thought of whom was ever present with me. Long, long had I accustomed myself to the idea that I should never see her again in this world. She had become my good angel—how, I cannot explain, for I hardly knew her. But as a cloud will sometimes take a shape while we continue to gaze at it, so did my imagination—building upon the few faint lines of reality—make for itself a complete picture of her.

I had been in my old home but a few days when I received a letter. It was written in English, and came from the Countess Mary.

"Dear Friend: I hear that you are with us for a short time. It is many years since we have met. If it be agreeable to you, I should like to see an old friend again. This afternoon I shall be in the Swiss cottage."

I lost no time in replying that I would wait upon her that afternoon.

The Swiss cottage formed a wing of the palace. About five o'clock I knocked at the door.

I had time to look round the room whilst I awaited the Countess. The sight of a number of familiar objects—things I had known in the old playroom of the castle—gave me a peculiar feeling. The pictures were new, but strange to say, just the same as those I had in my own apartment at the University. In one corner stood the Venus of Milo, which I had always held to be the finest statue of antiquity. Here, on the table, lay volumes of Dante, Shakespeare, Rückert's Poems, Carlyle, etc., just the same authors that I had on my own table. My meditations were interrupted by the opening of the door, and the Countess, reclining on her couch, was borne into the room.

What a vision! Her face remained calm as a lake until the bearers had retired. Then she looked at me— the old unfathomable glance — and each moment her face became more animated. "We are old friends," she said, "and I think we have not changed. I cannot say 'you,' and if I may not say 'thou,' we must talk English. Do you understand me?"

For such a reception I was not prepared. No masquerade this. Here was a soul that sought to speak to another soul; here was a greeting as when two friends cast aside their masks, and recognize each other. I clasped the hand that was held out to me.

How powerful is custom, and how hard is it even for related souls to speak the speech of nature! We both felt the embarrassment of the moment. I broke the silence by expressing what was passing through my mind:

"From their youth up men are accustomed to live in a cage, so that when they find themselves in the open air, they dare not trust their wings, from a vague fear that they are sure to knock against something."

"Yes," she replied, "and, to a certain extent, that is well. It seems as if it would be pleasant to live like the birds, and sing together on the branches, without having to be introduced to one another; but, my friend, there are owls and sparrows among the birds, and it is fortunate that we can pass these by as if we did not know them. Might not life be like poetry? The real poet puts beauty and truth into a certain form: ought not men to be their *real selves* whilst respecting a reasonable etiquette?"

I could not but recall Platen:

> "Denn was an allen Orten
> Als ewig sich erweist;
> Das ist in gebundenen Worten,
> Ein ungebundener Geist.

> "One thing in every quarter
> Itself eternal proves;
> Unbounded is the Spirit,
> Though, bound in words, it moves."

"Yes," said she. Then she continued, with a kindly and almost roguish smile, "One privilege comes of my invalid and retired life. I often heartily pity men and women that they can have no friendships with each other but they, or their relatives for them, must immediately think of love, or what people call love. Thereby they lose so much. Most women are hardly aware, perhaps, how much they might be helped through the converse of earnest, broad-minded men, and men would gain unspeakably in all knightly virtues and graces, had they opportunity for friendships with true gentlewomen."

She stopped with an expression of pain.

"I dare not talk more now," she said, "My doctor would not permit it. If I could hear a song of Mendelssohn's—the duet—you used to play long years ago."

As she folded her hands I saw on her finger the ring which she had once given to me, and which I had given back to her. For a moment I could not trust myself to speak, so at once sat down to the piano.

After playing a little, I looked at her and said:

"If only one could speak in sounds, without words!"

"And so one may," she answered. I have understood all. But to-day I am not able for more. We must grow accustomed to one another, and a poor, sick hermit may well count upon some indulgence. We meet to-morrow?"

I took her hand, and wished to raise it to my lips, but she held mine firmly, saying, "Better thus. Good night!"

FIFTH RECOLLECTION.

What I thought and felt as I walked home cannot be described. There are "thoughts without words" which each man must play for himself in his moment of intense joy or pain. I cannot say, however, that I felt either joy or pain, but only a rush of inexpressible surprise. Thoughts flew across my mind like shooting stars. As one may sometimes say to himself, "I am dreaming," so now I said, "I am awake; it is she!" Here, at last, was a soul fresh and clear as a spring morning. From the beginning, it seemed that she and I had recognized each other.

Now a delightful sort of life began. Every evening I spent with her. We were soon like old, intimate friends, and never thought of addressing each other but as "thou." I had once heard the greatest master of our time play upon the piano along with his sister, and could not understand how two persons could be so in sympathy as to give free course to their feeling, and not have the harmony disturbed. Now I understood it. Now I felt as if my own nature were not so very poor and empty, and that it had only required a little sunshine to

K

bring out its buds and blossoms. Yet, what a sad spring-time was this that came to her soul and mine! In May we forget that the roses fade so soon; but already each evening warned us that leaf after leaf was falling to the ground. She saw it sooner than I did, and spoke of it seemingly without pain. Each day our conversation grew more earnest, more solemn.

"I did not think," said she, one evening, as I was about to go away, "that I should live to be so old. When I gave you that ring on my confirmation day, I thought I must soon take leave of you. I have lived so many years and have enjoyed so much—and suffered so much—but one forgets that—and now, when I feel the hour of departure approaching, every moment is so precious. Good-night—to-morrow do not be too late of coming."

One morning as I entered her room, I found an Italian artist with her, and although it was plain that he was more artisan than artist, she spoke to him with a consideration and kindliness that showed her aristocracy of birth—her fineness of soul. As the artist took leave she said to me :—

"Now let me show you a picture that will give you pleasure. The original is in the gallery at Paris. I read a description of it, and have had this Italian make me a copy of it."

The picture was a middle-aged man, in old-German

costume. The expression was dreamy and resigned, and altogether so true, that one could not doubt that the man once lived.

"There is nothing better than a true human countenance," I said, "and not even a Raphael could have invented that one."

"No," said she. "I shall tell you why I wished to have this picture. I read that no one knew the artist, nor yet whom the portrait is intended to represent. Just such a picture I wanted for my gallery. For no one knows the author of the *Theologia Germana*, and we have therefore no picture of him. So I wished to try if a picture by an unknown artist of a person unknown, would pass for him. If you see no objection, we shall hang up this picture between the "Albigenses" and "The Diet of Worms," and call it the "German Theologian."

"Very good,' said I, "Only is it not too robust-looking for the Frankfort Doctor?"

"Perhaps," said she. "But for a suffering life like mine, there is much strength to be had from his book. When I read it I felt free to approve, or not, the old teacher, whoever he might be, for his doctrine had no outward compulsion for me, and, nevertheless, it took such a hold of me that for the first time I realized what revelation was. Religious teachers are apt to repel many of us, just because they would thrust revelation upon us, before the revelation has taken place within us. Often, often has that troubled me. Not that I ever doubted the divineness of our religion, but I felt that I had no right to a belief that had been handed to me, as it were; and that what I had received as a child, without understanding, could not actually belong to me. As if any one could believe for us, any more than they can live for us, or die for us! 'Truth makes revelation,' says some wise head, ' not revelation truth.' A godly man feels the divine ever present in him, although he is not always talking about it; he guards it secretly, as he would one of love's secrets. In my own being I feel often like that silver poplar before my window. You see it now, in the evening, quite still—not a leaf moving. But when the breeze of early morning touches it, the whole of its foliage will tremble, though stem and branches remain unshaken. The autumn comes, and every leaf is blown away, and withers; the stem and the branches stand, and await a new spring."

Her inward life seemed to be so under control that nothing could disturb her. Surely, hers was the better portion. Her conversation was simply thinking aloud, and what she said must have been the expression of thoughts that had long lived in her, for these were thrown out with the carelessness of a child throwing flowers from its lap. It distressed me that I could not open my soul to her in this same easy, spontaneous way. How few can open themselves freely! From the ceaseless deceptions that society forces upon them, with its customs, and its cautions, and its worldly wisdom, life becomes at last but a huge masquerade, and it is impossible, even when desired, to get back to the simple truthfulness that should be natural. Even love can hardly speak its own speech, far less maintain its own silence; but must rave and sigh and imitate the jargon of the poets. I would rather have confessed my love to her, but the words would not come. Before leaving I left with her a volume of Arnold's Poems, and asked her to read "The Buried Life." That was my confession. Then I knelt by the side of her couch, and said, "Good Night." "Good Night," said she, laying her hand upon my head, and the peace of her soul seemed to pass into mine. I walked away silently, and in the night I dreamed of a little silver-poplar around which the wind roared; but not one leaf moved in the branches.

SIXTH RECOLLECTION.

A knock came to my door early next morning, and my old doctor, the court physician, stepped in. He was not only a doctor, but a friend to the whole little city. He had seen two generations grow up. The children he had brought into the world were themselves fathers and mothers, and he looked upon them all as his own. He was unmarried. Though advanced in years, he had still a strong and handsome appearance. As a child I had the greatest faith in him; so much so that when I was ill, and my mother said she must send for the doctor, I felt that I was about to be made well; just as when the tailor was called for, I expected a new coat.

"How are you, my young friend?" said he, as he entered my room. "You do not look well; you must not study too much. However, I have no time to talk to-day, and only come to tell you not to go to see the Countess Mary again. I have been with her the whole night, and it is your fault. If you set store by her life, you will not go again. As soon as possible she must be taken away into the country somewhere. It would be well for you to travel awhile. Well, good morning; be prudent."

With these words he shook hands, and looked into my eyes with a significant expression, as if to extract a promise; then walked away to visit his sick children.

I was surprised beyond description to find that another had penetrated so far into the secret of my soul; to find that he knew what I myself hardly knew. My mind but just began to realize what he had said by the time that he was far down the street. Then I might compare myself to water that had long stood still by the side of the fire, but that suddenly boils up, and foams, and runs over.

Not to see her again! Not to see her again! I will be calm; I will not say a word; I will only stand near her window while she sleeps and dreams. But not see her again! Not bid her farewell!

Life is no idle play. Souls that fate has brought together may hold together. No power can part them if they have the courage of life and death. She cannot know that I love her. I hope nothing. My heart never beats so quietly as when I am by her side. What is it that we ask? Only that I may be her support in her suffering. and that she be my consolation or tender care till we reach the goal.

Every thought and hope of my soul fell back, like a bird that would soar into the blue sky, and does not see the wires that hem it in on every side. I was her guide and her friend. Would it be possible for her to regard me as more than that—she so far above me? Nerve thyself. Hast thou not, many a clear summer night in the woods, seen the moon's soft light reflected upon the dark ponds? So shines the Countess Mary upon thy dark life, and her calm light is reflected in thy heart; but— hope not a warmer ray!

Then her image seemed to stand before me. What harmony in her whole being! The beauty which nature gives with lavish hand does not please, unless it be part of the being. It offends rather. As when on the stage an actress enters in royal robes, showing in every step how far she herself is from being queenly. True beauty that palls not, lies in grace—the grace that is born of spirit,—that is the grace of the Countess Mary.

Thus, for I know not how long, did one thought chase another in a wild hunt. This was succeeded by a sort of calm that men call "after-thought," but which is rather "after-sight." Thoughts have had time to settle and take shape—quite a different shape often from what we expected. Our surprise is like that of the chemist who watches attentively the process of crystallization, and gets, somehow, a result quite other than he had anticipated.

The first words that I spoke when I roused myself for action were: "I must be off!" and then and there I wrote to the doctor that I would be absent for a fortnight, and that I left everything in his hands. That evening saw me on my way to the Tyrol.

SEVENTH RECOLLECTION.

To ramble with a friend through the valleys and over the mountains is refreshing to body and mind; but to go lonely and alone is nothing but weariness, and a squandering of time. How could I profit by the green hills, or the blue sea, or the mighty waterfall! Instead of my gazing at them, they gazed at me. One sad thought followed another, like a song that would not be got rid of. In the evening when I entered an inn and sat down exhausted, the people stared at me and queried who the lonely stranger could be. Then I would rush out into the dark night where no one could see my loneliness, and repeat over and over Schubert's song, "Yonder, where thou art not, yonder is happiness!" The calm, the order, the infinitude of nature, brought me a sort of resignation. I felt in me, and under me, and over me, the presence of a Power in whom the symbol becomes the reality, anxiety is changed to rest, and the *one* is transformed into the *all*.

Thus I pursued my way, sometimes happily, sometimes sadly; for even if we have been able to attain to a certain peace in our inner life, it is difficult to continue in our sanctuary,—difficult, too, if we forget it for a while, to find our way back to it.

Weeks went by, and not a syllable from her. If she had died without my taking leave of her, could I ever forgive myself? Alas! how men play with life: how they put off and off the best they might do, or enjoy, never realizing that each day may be their last, and that lost time is lost eternity! When I considered the words of the Doctor when I last saw him, and when I considered the step I had taken in making this sudden journey, I felt that I had not acted from a sense of duty but only from a feeling of pride. I had wished to show how firm I could be. It would have been harder to have made a confession to him, and to have remained. One duty rose clearly before me now,—to return to her at once, and bear whatever heaven might send. Just as I had planned my return, the Doctor's words recurred to me, "She must be taken away to the country." It was possible, nay, probable, that she might be at her castle, not far distant, where she herself told me she often passed the summer. In a day I could be there. I started with the first ray of the morning, and the evening found me at the castle.

A sentinel walked up and down before the door. I hurried up to him and learnt that the Countess Mary and her attendants were there.

A new life of reality seemed nigh; all that I had suffered began already to appear like a horrible dream. There are but few such moments in a man's life; thousands have never known this ecstacy. The mother who for the first time takes her child into her arms, the father who welcomes back from the war an heroic son, the poet who is crowned by his country—these understand what is meant by a dream becoming reality.

In the pale, evening light, I saw a white, reclining form, and a clear voice said,—each word falling like a cooling rain-drop after a hot summer day—" How oddly people meet!"

"How oddly they meet, and how oddly they lose themselves!" I answered the countess, hastily, and seized her hand. I felt that we were once more together, and unchanged.

"It is their own fault if they lose themselves," said she, and her voice, which accompanied her words like music, changed to a minor key.

"That is true," I replied. "Are you well? May I talk to you?"

"My dear friend," said she smiling, "I am always ill, as you know. If I say that I am well, it is only out of love for the old Doctor, who is convinced that I am alive only through his skill. But where have you been all this time that I have heard nothing of you? The doctor gave so many reasons for your abrupt departure, that at length I told him that I knew not what to think. The last reason that he gave compelled me to answer, that I understood neither him nor you. I am such a poor, frail piece of humanity that my life might rightly be called a lingering death. If Fate has sent two souls who understand me—who love me as the doctor expresses it—

wherefore should this disturb my peace or theirs? I could not help saying to our old friend, 'My dear Doctor, we have so many thoughts and so few words, that we have to crowd many thoughts into one word. If people unacquainted with us heard that my young friend loved me, and I him, they might think it was as Romeo loved Juliet, and Juliet, Romeo; and then you might be right in saying that it must not be. But, is it not true, my old Doctor, that you love me also, and I you; and I have loved you many years—though I may not have confessed it—yet I am neither despairing nor unhappy thereby. Listen, dear Doctor, I have more to say. I really believe that you have an unfortunate sort of affection for me, and that you are jealous of our young friend. Every morning do you not come to inquire for me, though you know that all is well. Do you not bring me the choicest flowers of your garden? Have I not had to give you my portrait? Did you not sit by my couch last Sunday when you thought I slept—O, I did not mean to speak of this—and let your tears fall upon my cheek as you sobbed, "Mary! Mary!" Ah! my dear Doctor, our young friend has never done that; yet, you have sent him away. As I thus spoke to him half earnestly, half jestingly, as I always do, I saw that I had hurt the old man. Then I took up a volume of Wordsworth—my favorite poet—which I had been reading, and said, 'Here is another old man whom I love with all my heart; who understands me, and whom I understand; yet, I have never seen him, nor ever shall see him—that is the way in this world. Let me read you a poem of his, that you may see how men can love, and how true love is a quiet blessing that the lover lays on the head of the loved one.' I read to him Wordsworth's ' Highland Girl.' Draw the lamp nearer, my friend, and read me the poem again, for it refreshes me as often as I hear it. A spirit breathes through it that is one with the calm of yonder sunset that is stretching out its loving arms over the snow-clad mountains."

She handed me the book, and I read the poem, and it was to me as a draught of fresh spring-water out of the cup of some great green leaf.

Then I heard her melodious voice, like the first rich tones of an organ rousing people from a dreamy prayer, repeating:

> "And I would have
> Some claim upon thee, if I could,
> Though but of common neighborhood.
> What joy to hear thee and to see
> Thy elder brother I would be,
> Thy father—anything to thee.''

" So I wish you to love me," said she, "and so does the old Doctor love me, and so we ought all, in one way or another, to love each other, and to have faith in each other. But the world— what little I have seen of it—seems not to understand this love or faith, nor to make any provision for it. Men have made of this earth, where all might have been so happy, a truly sorrowful existence, and the more high-minded and sensitive one is, the more must one feel it to be a vale of tears. Love seems to be nothing more for us than the prelude to the comedy or tragedy of marriage. Is there then really no other love now?"

She always spoke up, not down. The melody of her sentence was as when a child says, " Is it not so, father?" There was something so imploring in her voice that it was almost impossible to contradict her.

" One thing that I admired in Wordsworth," she continued, " is that he is *true*. He uses no exaggerated phrases. He is *true*, and does not all lie in that little, comprehensive word? He opens our eyes to the beauty that, like the daisy in the meadows, lies beneath our feet. The true poet seems to have a clear insight into the eternal. Scoffers may talk as they will, but it is just this superhuman element that moves the human heart. Who more able to speak of earthly beauty than Michael Angelo—and how? Because it was to him as a reflection of ideal perfection. We recollect his sonnet:

'La forza d' un bel volto al ciel mi spiona
(Ch.' altro in terra non è che mi diletti),
E vivo ascendo tra gli spirti diletti;
Grazia ch'ad nom mortal raro si dona,

TRANSLATIONS.

> Sì ben col suo Fattor l'opra consuona
>   Ch'a Lui mi levo per divin concetti;
>   E quivi informo i pensier tutti e i detti;
>   Ardendo, amando per gentil persona,
> Onde, se mai da due begli occhi il guardo
>   Torcer non so, conosco in lor la luce,
>   Che mi mostra la via, ch'a Dio mi guide;
> E so nel lume loro acceso io ardo,
>   Nel nobil foco mio dolce riluce
>   La gioja che nel cielo eterna ride.'

> A beauteous face illumined the way to Heaven;
> No more on earth is aught that can delight me;
> To spirits elect, uprising, I unite me—
> A grace to mortal man but rarely given.
> So well the work accords with Him who made it.
>   That unto Him it lifts me: my life's story
>   Is formed of thought and deeds, to suit its glory:
>   It did command me: I have but obeyed it.
> And if from these two eyes so brightly shining,
>   I turn not; but do recognize their fitness
>   To guide me still upon the path supernal;
> Enkindled at their fire, myself resigning
>   I shall reflect their lustre, and bear witness
>   To joy, that reigneth in the Heavens, eternal.

She was exhausted and ceased speaking, and I would not disturb the silence that ensued. When, after an intimate interchange of thought, human hearts feel at peace with each other, and there comes a solemn pause, we say that an angel flies through the room; and I could have fancied that I heard the light wings of the angel of peace over our heads. Whilst my glance rested upon her, it seemed as if she became transfigured in the soft twilight of that summer evening, and only her hand, which I held in mine, assured me of her bodily presence. I looked around and saw that the moon had risen in its full splendor between the two mountains opposite the castle, and its silvery beams were falling upon the lake. Never had nature appeared to me so lovely; never had I experienced such a deep peace, never had her face looked so angelic. "Mary," said I, "let me, such as I am, speak to you, as I have often wished to speak. At this moment when we feel so intensely the nearness of the superhuman, let out souls pledge themselves to each other, so that nothing may again separate us."

I knelt before her, and would have kissed her hand, but she drew it away with an expression of pain; then she raised herself with a deep sigh, and said:

"You have hurt me, but it is my fault. Enough for to-day. To-morrow evening I shall expect you."

Oh, where had all my heavenly peace in a moment fled! I saw how she suffered, and all that I could do was to call her attendant; and then, full of gloomy thoughts, make my solitary way home through the gloom.

LAST RECOLLECTION.

When I awoke next morning, the sun was shining over the mountains and in at my bedroom window. Was it the same sun that last evening watched us with a warm, lingering look, like a parting friend who wished to bless the union of our souls; and then sank like a last hope?

Was I the same man who a few hours before threw myself upon my couch, broken in spirit and body?

What would become of men without sleep? When this nightly messenger comes and closes our eyes, what guarantee have we that he will ever open them again—that he will bring us back to ourselves in the morning? It needed not a little courage on the part of the first man to yield himself to this untried benefactor. I doubt whether any one would, voluntarily, spite of fatigue, have entered this mysterious dreamland.

That which passed through my mind last night, like a heavy mist, now grew clearer, and my old energy revived. I was fully convinced that our souls belonged to each other, whether as brother and sister, parent and child, bridegroom and bride. We must now and forever remain near to each other. We had but to find the right name for that which in our stammering speech is called love.

> "Thy elder brother I would be,
> Thy father—anything to thee!"

It was for this *anything* that a name had to be found; for the world, clumsy and savage yet, acknowledges nothing without a name. She had herself said that she loved me with that universal love which is the source of all other. Her displeasure when I confessed my love to her, was unintelligible to me—but that could not destroy my firm belief in our mutual affection. Why try to fathom other minds, when we cannot fathom our own! All these reflections had such a consoling influence upon me, that, at length, not the smallest cloud appeared upon the sky of my future.

In this composed state of mind I was stepping out of the house, when I encountered a messenger with a letter. It came from the countess, and said: "To-morrow comes the Doctor; therefore, come the day after."

Two days out of my book of life! They had to be lived through, somehow. I resolved to pass them in making a record of all the beautiful thoughts that I had heard her utter—thoughts she had entrusted to me. Thus I lived in the remembrance of happy hours spent with her.

Together again! Be calm; murmur not; ask nothing; you are welcome; do not think ill of me. All this was expressed in her face when I saw her at our next meeting.

"Have you had a letter from the Doctor?" was her first question.

"No," I answered.

"My friend," she said, "we see each other for the last time. I have done you a great wrong—I feel that. I know the world so little. I thought a poor, frail being like myself could not have inspired more than pity. I have been so happy in your society. But the world does not understand love like mine—nor allow it. The old Doctor has opened my eyes. Believe me, I deeply grieve for what I have done. Can you forgive me? I trust we can part friends."

She closed her eyes to hide from me the gathering tears.

"Mary," I said, "for me there is but one life, and that is with you; but, also, one will, and that is yours; I am not ashamed to confess it; I love you and cannot think of you as apart from my love and care. You stand far above me in rank—in everything; and I can hardly grasp the thought of ever calling you my wife. But the world gives us no other way by which we can pass through life together."

"Men wander here on earth like the stars in heaven," she said. "They meet, and they part; and when the moment of parting comes, resistance is vain. It is impossible to understand; we can but trust. I cannot myself understand how my love for you can be wrong; no, I cannot, will not call it wrong; but—it must not be."

I could not give up the struggle so easily. "Let us see," I said, "to *whom* we owe this sacrifice. If our love was in contradiction to a higher law, I would, like you, bow in acquiescence. But, what opposes our love?

Nothing, really, but the idle babble of an unthinking, ignorant crowd. I wish to respect the laws of our society, but sometimes its false gods demand too great a sacrifice. Like the Athenians, we send each year a heavily-laden ship of youths and maidens as tribute to the monster who rules over society. There is hardly a heart that has not been broken, hardly a man of true feeling who has not had to break the wings of his love before it would fit in society's cage. When I think of my friends, I could tell you whole volumes of tragedies. One loved a maiden, and was loved by her. He was poor; she was rich. Angry relations stepped between them, and two hearts were broken. Why? Because the world holds it a misfortune for a lady to wear a dress made from the wool of a plant in America, and not from the fibres of a worm in China.

"Another loved a maiden and was loved again" He was Protestant; she was Catholic. The priests stepped between them and two hearts were broken.

"A third loved a maiden and was loved in return. He was patrician, she was plebian. Her sisters were jealous and caused dissension, and two hearts were broken.

"Collectors of statistics say—and I believe with truth —that every hour a heart is broken. Why? Because, in most cases, the world will acknowldge no love between strangers, unless they become man and wife. Can we not love a maiden without wishing to marry her? Alas, the world has turned the holiest we have in life into the commonest. You shut your eyes. Perhaps I have gone too far. But, enough, Mary; let us preserve one sanctuary where two hearts may speak the pure language of the heart, unmoved by the tumult of the world. The best portion of the world itself honors the heroic stand that noble hearts, conscious of their rectitude, oppose to its unrighteous—even if customary—customs. Do thou follow the dictates of thine own mind and heart!"

"And why dost thou love me?" she said, slowly, as if she must somehow delay the moment of decision.

"Why? ask the sun why it shines; ask the child why it is born. Your suffering shall be my suffering, and we shall bear it together—as a ship carries the sails that bear it into harbor."

"Then take me as I am," she said, "and may we be re-united in a brighter life."

Time stood still for us; the outward world had vanished. At length she whispered, "Now leave me alone. I cannot bear more. May we meet again, my friend—my beloved!"

These were the last words I heard her speak. I went home. At night the Doctor entered my room and said, "our angel has flown. Here is her last greeting." It was the ring. There was a piece of paper wound around it, with the words, "What is thine, is mine," the words I had used as a child. We sat a long time without speaking. The burden of sorrow seemed too heavy for us to bear. The old Doctor rose at last, saying, "I knew a soul as fair as hers. It was her mother's. I loved her mother, and her mother loved me. I sacrificed my happiness to my affection for her. I left home, and wrote to her that I released her from her engagement. I knew that our Prince loved her well. He married her, and I never saw her again till at her death-bed. She died at the birth of her daughter. You know, now, why I loved Mary. She was the only being that bound me to earth. Bear life as I have borne it. Help men; thank God that you have known such a one as she; that you have had the privilege of knowing and of loving her."

"We must submit," was all I was able to utter. And we parted for ever.

Days, and weeks, and months, and years, have flown. My native land is strange to me; the land of the stranger is my home. Her love has remained ever present with me; and, as a tear drops into the sea, so my love for her has fallen into the great sea of humanity, and embraces millions—millions of those very "strangers" whom it has been my lot from early childhood to love so well.

* * * * * * * * *

Only on serene summer days like this, when I throw myself down on the green grass in the woods, and feel that I am lonely and alone, there comes a movement in the churchyard of memory; omnipotent love asserts it self, and my heart cries out for the gentle being, who once turned on me her lustrous, far-seeing eyes, and I forget my love for the millions, in my love for one,— my good angel—and my thoughts are dumb, before the problem of finite and infinite Love.

WITHOUT A MOTHER.

Translated from the German.

To-day, as I watched the first snow fall, and observed at the same time the thinly clad, poverty-stricken children, with pale, melancholy faces, go by, there came to my remembrance a touching incident that happened in my boyhood, and left an impression upon my mind never to be effaced.

It was the history of a girl and a boy—twins, who, one bleak, frosty morning, went away "to seek a mother," and who, a few days afterwards, were found in a wood, frozen to death.

I had known the two children well—the dark-complexioned Mali, whose thick braids of hair fell over her shoulders, and the fair Conrad, with his honest blue eyes. Often had I gone strawberrying with them, or with them chased the butterflies; and in winter we had snowballed each other, or had gone out with our little sleds together. As they were both pretty, and always neat and clean, notwithstanding their poverty, everybody looked at them with admiration. Their mother had died at their birth, and the father, a day laborer, who lived mostly by splitting wood—was a rough sort of man, who, in despair over his unhappy circumstances, fell into intemperate habits.

One morning the father was found dead in his bed. The poor twins were in a bewildered state of mind. Shivering in a room without a fire, they discussed, in childish fashion, what was to be done. Often had they heard the passers-by say: "These poor children, if only they had a mother!" And the already thoughtful Mali —for girls are more precocious than boys—had asked one of the neighbors, "What do they mean by 'a mother?'"

The neighbour said in reply to the little girls inquiry, "A mother is a woman who takes care of little children as the apple of her eye; one is never cold, but always warm and comfortable when one has a mother."

The little girl carried this answer to her brother, and as they sat together at the bare table, a bright idea seemed to fill Mali's mind, and she said: "Do you know what Conrad? Father is dead, so there is nobody now to care anything about us, unless it be cross old Hanna. Let us go away and search for a mother. There are such lots of mothers in the world; surely there must be one for us somewhere!"

Conrad had nothing to say against the proposal, and was ready without much preparation; but Mali stuck a piece of bread in her pocket, and hung by a cord, round her neck, a woollen muff. Thus, hand in hand, they passed out at their doorway, through the streets, and followed the footpath across the meadows until they arrived at the wood. Some of the country-people saw them, and one man asked them, in a tone of surprise, what they wanted going through the snow this cold weather. They replied they were "seeking for a mother." The man shook his head, and watched them awhile, until they disappeared among the trees. As they entered the wood and saw the pines glistening in winter apparel, they thought it must be Christmas there, for these trees were exactly like what the rich people had in their houses on Christmas day. They could not sufficiently admire the loveliness of it all; and they had a hearty laugh when they shook the fir-tree and a whole shower-bath of snow fell down upon them and filled their eyes.

On they went, Mali stopping now and then to call out in an imploring voice: "Mother! Mother!" Her own voice sounded in reply, and frightened a woodpecker, which flew upward, scattering the snow from the branches of the trees as it went. Continuing their way up the hill, they came to a diverging path by which they stopped and gazed at the rosy evening light tinging the tops of the firs. By this time they began to feel very weary, so sat down under the shelter of a pine tree to rest. Mali produced the bread from her pocket, and gave it to her brother. The cold made their fingers numb, and Mali took Conrad's hands in her own and drew them into her muff. Then sleep overcame them, and they slumbered, hand in hand, and cheek to cheek.

Suddenly, as if touched by a warm ray of light, Mali awoke, and waking her brother, she said to him: "Conrad, I begin to feel warm and comfortable; can it be the mother?" "Yes," whispered Conrad, "It is the mother!" And in closer embrace they fell asleep smiling, and opened their eyes no more. Our old mother, Earth, whose hard exterior permits us but to suspect her love, had opened her arms in compassion and taken the twins to herself.

THE DEATH OF RAFAEL.

Translated from the German.

Cardinal Bibieno describes to his niece Maria (the affianced bride of Rafael), in a letter, the death of the immortal master, as follows :—

"Out of a twofold night—a darkened earth and a darkened soul—I send to thee these lines. The wreath which our dear friend on that memorable evening handed to thee lies withered, like himself. It lies like a symbol of resignation at the foot of the crucifix, before which thou prayest daily. That painful presentiment of thine has been fulfilled. Rafael has left us. Thou, who wert appointed to be a true companion unto him, art now the bride of Heaven. Rafael is dead! His burning soul consumed all that was mortal of him, leaving to us only that which is immortal. Good Friday was his birthday: it is also the day of his death. In the flower of life and in the midst of happiness to have been thus snatched away!

"When I think of all that he did in these seven and thirty years for the glory of the Church and of the nation, I am filled with devout reverence for the human soul. Look at the picture of the Madonna which he but recently painted for the monastery of the holy Sixtus in Piacenza; look into the eyes, into the eyes of the young Saviour. It was painted, like any other picture, by means of the hand and the brush ; but the sublimity of the heavens meets you in these eyes. He who had the power to paint them belonged no more to this earth.

"My letter of yesterday informed you that for three days we feared the worst. Rafael himself was the most composed among us. He spoke of time and eternity with the utmost calm. Then, having tried to comfort us, he made his will. As I walked this evening from his Holiness to Rafael's dwelling, a soft light and a sweet fragrance seemed to fill the air. The peace of God had fallen upon the solemn City of Rome ; and, as I entered the house, hope was renewed within me, and I felt strengthened.

"In the sick chamber, I found Count Castiglione, the father's Antonio and Domenico, the painter Giulio, and others. Rafael's couch had been moved to the window, which stood wide open. Never before had Rafael appeared so beautiful. Could it have been the effect of the evening light, or was it his near victory over earth ? The skin was more transparent, the brown artist-eyes more brilliant than ever. He was holding some spring flowers, but laid them to one side when I handed to him thy wreath of roses. Then he raised the cross to his lips as he murmured, 'Maria.' Though his voice was clear, the words seemed breathed rather than spoken. I communicated to him the message sent by his Holiness: 'Dear Rafael, let the sympathy of the highest as well as of the lowest be to thee a motive to linger longer among us.' He smiled mournfully.

"Castiglione then spoke: 'Thou *shalt*, thou *must* live. Through that which thou hast done hast thou awakened in us the desire for that which thou canst accomplish. Thy favorite thought—that ancient Rome with its palaces and marble temples, its triumphal arches and statues be reconstructed—is not yet realized.'

"'Yes, I wished it rebuilt,' answered he; 'and, if God had granted me longer life, my wish would have been realized.'

"'Do not speak,' said I, almost reproachfully, 'as if hope were vain.'

"'Father,' replied he, 'to leave this earth is not easy to me. Could I but describe to you the longing which takes hold of me as the daylight disappears! My soul clings to yonder sunbeam which lingers upon the hill. How beautiful is the world! How lovely is the human countenance! Ah! to take leave of all this without a hope of awaking on the morrow!' 'Beloved,' cried I, 'forget not that the Saviour died, that we are going from the darkness of earth to meet an eternal day.' 'How could I forget that?' said he; 'but the earth is wonderfully beautiful!'

"A pause ensued. Castiglione took hold of Rafael's hand, while the latter gazed through the open window to the hill upon which the soft radiance of the departing day seemed to rest. Then turning his glance upward to where Hesperus like a messenger of heaven shone, 'I shall see Dante!' he exclaimed.

"At this moment, some one drew the curtain from Rafael's last picture, the 'Transfiguration.' We wept aloud as we looked at the immortal work of the mortal hand. Rafael's features changed suddenly. He began to speak with difficulty. Twice I heard that saying of Plato's, 'Beautiful is the reward of victory, and hope is great.' He supposed that thou wert present, and begged thee to lay thy hand upon his forehead. Giulio threw himself down upon the couch, and sobbed aloud. I called upon all to kneel and to pray for the passing soul. Helped by two of us, he raised himself, and, with his now lustreless eyes staring into vacancy, asked 'Where does the sun shine from?' 'Rafael,' I cried, 'do you know me? How do you feel?' At first, he appeared not to have heard. Then he whispered, 'Happy.' The peaceful expression of his countenance corroborated the speech. He said no more but quietly passed through the final struggle.

"Night had come, when the long, solemn stillness was broken by the words, 'He is dead!'"

ADDITIONAL POEMS

SONG.

Tender little rose-bud,
    Rosy-red to-day ;
Fading little rose-bud,
    Falling by the way ;
Dying little rose-bud,
    Gone, alas ! for aye.

Feathery little snow-flake,
    Starry pure to-day ;
Melting little snow-flake,
    Falling by the way ;
Dying little snow-flake,
    Gone, alas ! for aye.

Oh ! the pretty rose-bud,
    Once so bright and gay ;
Oh ! the starry snow-flake,
    Dying by the way ;
Memory is planting
    Her own flowers to-day.

HYMN.

O Reason, Wonder, Doubt
    Great warriors three!
    A trinity
No true-soul lives without.

Reviled, ye still endure
    In every land—
    A stalwart band
To keep the conscience pure.

To-day the tyrant king
    Shall crouch before
    Your temple-door;
He knows the spell you bring.

Immortal spirits all!
    Iniquity
    And calumny,
Though others they appal,

Your might cannot subdue,
   Who only rise
   With clearer eyes
To wage the fight anew—

The battle for the sway
   Of liberty,
   Fraternity,
And light of the new day!

SONG.

Forget-me-not and clover,
   And violet in the grass,
How smilingly you greet me
   Wherever I may pass!

As happy as the sunshine!
   From every trouble free!
Alas, could I but join too
   In nature's jubilee!—

You envy not each other
   Content each in its place
A living lesson are you
   Unto the human race!

THE COMRADES.

Those bright first days of June, how happy they!
    We followed all the windings of the stream—
My comrade with his sketch-book in his hand,
    I, with my songs. A far-off, waking dream

It seems to-day. As on and on we roved,
    Sweet converse was not wanting: for we thought
How life might be sublime—a something far,
    Far loftier than all the schools had taught.

Men's souls, we said, must grow to more and more
    And sin, at last, and sorrow, disappear;
And everyone be free to work from love,
    And speak the truth by instinct, without fear.

And one and other quoted Emerson,
    And Plato and Aurelius, wise and true,
Rejoicing as we thought what man had done,
    What it were possible for man to do.

And oft, absorbed in solemn revery,
    We wandered on in silence many a mile,
Till suddenly to consciousness recalled,
    I sang an old-time ditty to beguile

The way. And when the song was done,
    My dreaming comrade would keep up the strain
And whistle, clear and low and plaintively,
    And o'er and o'er again, the same refrain.

It was the 'Loreley' those calm June days
    That caught his fancy. Youthful still and glad
He went about repeating the weird lay,
    "I know not what it means, I am so sad!"*

'Twas thus we lived from day to day until
    One morning fair when he rowed out to sea—
To get a distant view he was intent—
    Too far away, he feared, it was for me.

---

* "Ich weiss nicht was soll es bedeuten
Dass ich so traurig bin."—*Heine.*

"But watch at eve," he cried, "by setting sun,
  For swiftly then I will return— Good-bye!
Farewell, my little comrade, for a day!"
And then he pushed off, whistling 'Loreley.'

The day grew darker—darker every hour;
  The 'Loreley' took root within my brain;
A thunder-storm arose; the lightning flashed;
  I hurried through the wind, and storm, and rain,

And down the rocky shore. The sun had set;
  My comrade must be on his homeward way.
No star appeared that night upon the sky;
  And never boat came up into the bay.

"Star to star vibrates light; may soul to soul
Strike through a finer element of her own?"
                              —*Tennyson.*

I sat all alone, in the gloom of the night, with the dead
  A stranger I found myself there, and in a strange land,
And this way and that the crowd hurried past, but I knew
  Not one face, and I said, there is none who would
    understand!

Then I took up my pen that was lying close by at my side,
  And wrote the strange story of him whose body lay near,
And I carried the body away to its home in the earth,
  Whilst I pondered life's mystery, what meaneth
    'there' and what 'here.'

Returning at length to the spot where the body had lain,
  I left the sad history—as it had flowed from my pen;
Then onward afar through the wide world I wandered away,
  Still mourning the fate of the one who had passed
    from 'mong men.

It chanced (what is chance?) that one morning a stranger approached—
  A stranger who said, " I would speak with you : some how you seem
As if you were meant for the hero of something I read—
  A story that touched me long since, like a terrible dream."

Therewith he related, so feelingly, I could have wept
  The history which I had written, so far, far away,
And left in the place where I watched by the side of the
    dead—
An outburst of grief for the one who was buried that
    day.

SONNET

Mysterious life! we speak as if we knew
  What meant this vortex: Ah, what doth it mean?
  A spirit of unrest is Life—hath been
  Alluring male with many-tinted hue.
From darkest chasm it lifts man to a peak
  Where he may see ideal flowers blow;
  But as he learns to love them, it will show
  Him other heights that he is forced to seek.
Enchantress, Disenchantress,—both in one
  Surrounding us to-day with dazzling light,
  To-morrow hiding every ray of sun
Till we are sunk in the abyss of night.
  The oracles are dumb: what'er Life be,
  Man walks by faith alone; he cannot see.

SONNET.

Still, still thy waters now, thou rippling rill
   That oft hast cheered my mornings with thy song;
   The icicles, pure, crystal-like and long
   Are hanging from the boulders. Ah, how chill
And bleak and brown, the glassy slope whereon
   I've sat and watched the rushes long and lank
   Swayed by the wind until they broken sank
   On thy bright stream. Oh, for the summer gone!
Oh, for a blink of sunshine yet to wake
   The melody stored in that heart of thine,
   And let thee ripple onward as of old!
I would the sun shone warm, not for thy sake
   Alone, but man's too: e'en his song divine
   Too oft, alas! is hushed through frost and cold.

SONNET.

Poor, little bird, within thy narrow cage!
    Sad-eyed from pining for the forest-glade,
    And swaying boughs, and fragrant woodland shade,
    How hast thou failed of thine own heritage!
To dip thy wing in ocean's briny wave,
    And fly from cliff to cliff, and coast to coast,
    O'er sea and land, with a companion host,—
    All this was thine by right. Ah, could I save
Thee yet! Rememberest thou thy native hills
    Beyond th'horizon and the sea-girt rocks?
    Quit this dull prison-house and all its ills,
Thy melancholy song here only mocks
    Us all. Sweet rover, there—I ope the door!
    The world is all before thee—upward—soar!

SONNET.

Swift roll the waters of thy mighty stream
   Between low banks, white with new-fallen snow;
   The island yonder intersects the flow,
   And sparkles underneath a sudden gleam
Of golden light. Like sportive butterflies
   Appear the white-winged boats that dot the lake;
   One almost might suppose they could partake
   In man's enjoyment—spirits in disguise!
Against a gnarled and hoary oak I lean,
   And see the play of life surrounding me—
   The buoyant, tossing waves of purest green,
O'erhead the sparrows twittering in their glee.
   How can the world, I marvel, be so glad,
   While in my soul it is so dark and sad!

SONNET.

Wait, trusting heart ! A little while ago
    The purple fruit was hanging on the vine ;
    To-day we seek in vain for any sign
    Of life—deep-buried now beneath the snow.
A violet pale, that looked with anxious face
    Around the garden bare, where once had bloomed
    The tender rose, is now itself entombed,
    And no green thing survives to mark the place.
Our mother, Nature, lies enwrapt in sleep,
    Nor dare we interrupt her happy dream ;
    The loving sky above her, watch doth keep,
    And things are not at all what now they seem.
    Already man's quick fancy sees the rose,
    And violet, too, their new spring-buds disclose.

SONNET.

Those poor, dumb brutes —what slaves of them we make!
    Inflicting on them a too ponderous load;
    Unheeding, though they faint, we onward goad
    Them to their death—and all for our own sake.
Of massive body as compared with man,
    What could they not accomplish with their strength
    If but to thought allied! They might at length
    Reverse the order—lead creation's van!
Yet man himself is slave unto some soul
    Whose keener sight, unwitting, leads him on;
    The thoughtless multitude moves as a whole,
And rarely know its leader till he's gone.
    Thought sways the world; *it* is the true real head;
    The king's thought rules, although the king be dead!

SONNET.

With hopefulness man tills the fruitful ground,
    And wanders o'er the globe both far and wide
    Counting the harvest rich it shall provide—
The varied wealth in which it doth abound.
O toiler on the land, or on the sea,
    Or in the mine, or high on throne of state,
    While thou art seeking gold at every gate,
Be loyal to the spirit-god in thee.
What earthly bloom can be compared to this—
    The image in thy soul—the immortal tree,
    Igdrasil—symbol of man's two-fold bliss,
Whose roots encompass earth from sea to sea.
    Its towering stem is lost to mortal sight,
    Its foliage mingles with th' Eternal Light!

SONNET.

The young moon rises, glimmering through the pines
   And now above the river glides aloft,
   Its radiant beams descending pure and soft
   Across the peaceful sky, in silvery lines.
Bright orb! These spiritual rays can bind
   The earth to thee—those ties so beautiful,
   So tender, delicate and dutiful,
   Embracing all like gentle summer wind.
Now higher, higher, climbing ever higher,
   Thy glance fills all the chamber where I write;
   Yet, strange as it may seem, thy heavenly fire
I can reject—say "Not for me to-night!"
   Though queen thou reignest over sea and land,
   I shut thee off at will with this frail hand!

SONNET. (Addressed to a Poet.)

"Ich zieh' mich in mein Inneres still zurück,
. . . . . .
Du, meine Welt."—CHAMISSO.

Prize thou the kingdom of thy solitude—
    A monarch there if thou art fit to reign;
    It shall become to thee a vast domain
    Beyond the reach of earth's vicissitude.
Though 'mid the endless turmoil of the street,
    Outstripped thou art by a too heartless race,
    Yet, nobly, shalt thou with thy thought keep pace,
    Treading the ideal path with firm-set feet.
Nor shalt thou hope from earth a recompense—
    No richer art thou for a worldly prize;
    The true wealth is contained in the sweet sense
Of dignity of Truth without disguise:
    And this no earthly power can wrest from thee,
    King of thyself—thy land of liberty!

SONNET.

"Good-night! Farewell!" The hour is here at last.
    The clock strikes twelve! faint—fainter comes the
        sound!
    'Farewell' in bygone days was never found
    So doleful: now we stand and look aghast!
Of solemn aspect everything has grown;
    The room and all its objects seem resigned,
    As if they, too, were burdened with a mind
    Bewailing joys that have forever flown.
The waves of hope are rolling to our shores,
    Receding billows sigh as if pain;
    Man's buoyant spirit ever upward soars,
Though, disappointed, it may sink again—
    But hark! a joyful peal! a matin-bell!
    A happy New Year, friends, and not farewell!

FINIS.

www.ingramcontent.com/pod-product-compliance
Lightning Source LLC
Chambersburg PA
CBHW020910230426
43666CB00008B/1386